FACES
A Tribute To Marworth

By

Cliff W.

Sobriety Press Publishing

Edited by **Pamela Wilson and Gordon H.**

Cover Design by **Cliff W.**

Produced by **SOBRIETY PRESS PUBLICATIONS**

ISBN **0-939847-02-7**

Library of Congress # **87-90594**

Printed in The United States of America

Production Consultant, **Julius J. Wilson**

SOBRIETY PRESS
P.O. Box 201
Washington, New Jersey 07882

This book is available at a special discount when ordered in bulk quantities.

DEDICATION

This book I dedicate to my Higher Power, God as I understand Him, for without Him in my life, my mind, body, and soul would simply be void any real true purpose, period.

To Nick, Gordon, Cheryl, and the entire Marworth Family, for without their direct input, direction, and unconditional love, I may not have attempted this project at all.

To my wife Pamela for the many, many sacrifices she has made in my behalf, besides leading me to Marworth to regain my sanity and consciousness. Also my mother and children along with Julius and the rest of my family.

To all my fellowship which have become my life, my love, and my conscious communication to end with my Higher Power.

To all above, I most humbly offer and send my most enthusiastic gratitude and thanks.

In Recovery,

Cliff W.

TABLE OF CONTENTS

ALL WALKS OF LIFE

Alcohol drafts people from all walks of life, of all ages, of both
sexes, of all morals;
Alcohol enters the lives of all the peoples on earth, with its
passport it travels the entire world.
Alcohol is a vicious disease destroying its prey, under the guise
of many different faces;
Alcohol has no preference of life striking all the levels, it flows
in the gutters and in the highest places.
Alcohol contracts some personally making them alcoholics,
enlisting them to serve death and decay;
Alcohol wittingly reflects all the shame, pain, and guilt, its
victims aim the blame the other way.
Alcohol speaks every language in the world fluently, it's voice is
fully heard and strongly understood;
Alcohol controls your mind by submerging it in denial, you
wouldn't be disloyal to it even if you could.
Alcohol is color blind which it uses to its advantage, to
camouflage its movements and its direction;
Alcohol uses insanity as a weapon to induce other chemicals
and drugs, while you're in a state of depression.
Alcohol will quench your thirst with mad hot tingling liquids,
nutritiously good and healthy nourishment?
Alcohol resides in the best of homes, resorts, and castles, first
class all the way and not pay a cent.
Alcohol will take the bread and milk from the mouths of babies,
forsaking clothing, shelter, and care;
Alcohol in politics is a dictator and there are never any
elections, its demands are heavy to bare.
Alcohol at social events rises to capture the spot light, its ego
and pride demands first prize;

Alcohol can turn a strong man into an airless wimp balloon, as
his family watches with tears in their eyes.
Alcohol will take your faith in God locking it up in a bottle,
reflecting that faith back unto you;
Alcohol can make you think and act as if you're truly a genius,
but outside of drinking what really can you do?
Alcohol will carve you in slices as you would a holiday turkey,
and never, not once use a knife;
Alcohol will blanket your logic and smother your understanding;
thank God we have A.A. for all walks of life.

INTRODUCTION

The writings throughout this book are a direct result of the blessings, gifts, and insights that my Higher Power, God has revealed unto me. It is my only choice to refer to God as I understand Him as my Higher Power.

I am in pursuit of sharing my new awareness of life, through poetry, to all the peoples on all levels of the general public throughout our society. I am a very grateful recovering alcoholic, and I carry the message also through this gift I have received.

For over twenty-one years I helplessly bore countless negative situations, pain, and tears from my disease of alcoholism. I was too afraid to ask any questions, I lacked the confidence, and the use of basic common sense to attempt to seek positive direction. Most of all, I truly felt in my heart that I had fell "beyond" the grasp of God's forgiving grace.

Through a positive rehabilitation program, my deep renewed enthusiastic faith, and two years of actively and successfully arresting my alcoholism through A.A. I can now see vividly in retrospect optimistically the true natures of many of my past shortcomings.

Today I have an emotional awareness and understanding of life that I never knew existed beyond two years ago, and I must share it to keep it.

I truly and honestly feel I have been commissioned by my Higher Power to record these writings, thus I am merely a secretary.

These works are totally independent in every aspect of Alcoholics Anonymous—A.A. The references to A.A. in this book are my personal views and feeling. I truly *know* that the A.A. program has most definately saved my life, in every aspect of the word. Enjoy your reading.

In Recovery,

Cliff W.

WHAT IS AN ALCOHOLIC?

An alcoholic is a person who has contracted a very deadly disease,
so cunning, baffling, and powerful, even the strongest are forced on their knees.
An alcoholic is a person being driven by an authority beyond human control,
without passion, it will push you into a burning fire; without pity, it has no heart or soul.

An alcoholic is a person who must consume every drop to be gotten from the glass,
out of all the words in our language we use, when offered a drink we can't say I'll pass.
An alcoholic lives in an illusion constantly, and thinks the world is wrong but he's right.
In every confrontation they're faced with, their first and last resort is to fight.

An alcoholic is employed by alcohol, and works out in a town called insanityville;
there they mass produce many marketable products, even I've heard of death, destruction, and kill.
An alcoholic is a person who lies in the gutter, who searches garbage cans and has no poise,
who lost the home, job, and family who rides through town in a new Rolls Royce.

An alcoholic is a very stubborn person, trusting in only the strength of his illness itself;

when feeling weak, sad, and low he knows where to go to get his beef; it sits on the shelf.
An alcoholic is usually shy, encircled in loneliness, too frightened to reach or ask for help,
roaming night and day in sheer misery, afraid if once standing in the sun he would melt.

An alcoholic is a person whose freedom has been forbidden, whose will has been taken away,
who is a slave chained to darkness, who is considered to have no real mentality.
An alcoholic to me means A.A., growing and striding together every second, minute and hour.
Through humility I feel like a newborn babe; my nourishment is faith in my Higher Power.

PROGRESSIONISM

My first involvement with alcohol, was drinking out of curiosity.
I was just a child dancing with danger, all done so innocently.
My parents said beer is good for you, it has vitamins and minerals and is filling.
I thought of it as being nutritious, when it came to beer I would always be willing.
For years I sipped on my mother's beer, I can't remember ever getting indigestion.
I do remember going from sips to a glassful, never realizing the creeping progression.
As a teen I began drinking independently, still beer was the drink of my choice.
Drinking was the rule at parties, at school, in my neighborhood hanging out with the boys.
The joyous euphoric sensation, I thought it was beautiful, really beyond my imagination.

I wanted to love, to hold, to grow with this sensation, losing all
of life's perception.
The tighter I held on, the weaker I became, totally beyond my
previous extensive education.
By adding drugs I thought I was strengthening my grip, unaware
as to in what direction.
Through loneliness and fear I developed rejection, which
brought hate and anger inside of me.
Through years I've stumbled in the darkness, and no one could
have told me it was insanity.
I remember the laughter upon approaching the sensation, I
remember the tears as it faded away.
Distorted I thought, there is no true God; I put him to the test,
He wouldn't let me feel this way.
In this hell I dwelled, relentlessly smashing all of my morals
and the mores of the land.
All my instincts from God, all the manners from my parents, all
the laws made to govern men.
Through the grace of God I was led into A.A., spiritually and
emotionally, my life was in shambles.
Now I have God, I have comfort, I have serenity, I have love, I
have A.A., it is with these I dare not gamble.

THE FIRST 90 DAYS

I've been shown a new life, so beautiful in so many ways.
A life I've adopted and learned to love during the past 90 days.
I thank God for all my blessings and gifts, to Him every day I
pray.
I thank God for all the people I've joined, I thank God for A.A.
Never did I ever imagine the genuine treasures A.A. would
bring.
The honesty, the love, the fellowship; it is to these I choose to
cling.

That strong helping hand of A.A., the one always vividly clear;
snatched me from darkness and insanity; humbly, I'm so grateful to be here.
All the garbage within from the past that my fear convinced me to tow,
was merely confusion based on delusion, making it impossible for me to grow.
Weakness, sadness, rejection, frustration, and hate were my community;
Now, hope, attraction, joy, satisfaction, and trust, A.A. has given to me.
My higher Power guided me into A.A., His reasons I won't ask why,
I'm too busy being a real human being, to entertain the thought in my mind.
As I start my day working through the steps of A.A., I feel a spiritual sense of power.
As I face things I can't change or would like to rearrange, there's no barrier His will can't tower.
The gratitude I feel from the humility I feel is really a joyous euphoric revelation.
Being reacquainted with my Higher Power through you, gives me a lovely serene sensation.
Today I began my second 90 day span, of the many more to come down the line;
Sobriety I can't buy nor obtain anyway I try, except by taking it one day at a time.

SOBRIETY VS SOBRIETY

I have years in this program; in fact, I can count the days.
With all the pressure I had on me, against the odds, I made it anyway.
I've got eight years, seven months, one week, and four days, of not drinking.

Always attending all the meetings, always paying attention and thinking.
I don't do much speaking or talking, I'm shy, but I know what's being said.
I ask God for forgiveness every night in my prayers before I go to bed.
Yes, I do sit in the back but I'm not hurting, it's just a habit I've developed over the years.
This program has made my life so happy, I can't remember the last time I shed tears.
No, I don't go to meetings every night anymore, during the week I make two or three.
But when I do go, I drop a two dollar bill in the basket, they always know it's me.
I work on the steps every Thursday, that's the meeting I haven't missed in years.
I'm on my fifth time around through the steps; the one I like best is the one on fears.
You know, I'm lucky, I never did have a sponsor, it's surprising I made it this long.
Well the fact is, I never had to fall in the gutter, I never did too many things wrong.
In the beginning I would ride with other guys to meetings; we were all so positive.
Now I ride alone when I go to meetings these days, there's no members where I live.
When I'm faced with a problem I can't handle, I know just what step to look for the solution.
I go get myself to a meeting, say my prayers that night, and ask God to mend my imperfections.
Yes, I've been here a long time and have long sobriety; oops running late, see you next week, gotta go.
If there's ever anyway I can help you or if you need a sponsor, don't hesitate, just let me know.

THE POWER OF GOD THROUGH A.A.

While going down for the third time, drowning in the sea, in panic and blindness; I reached out, A.A. rescued me.
I had my wrist outstretched, with razor in my other hand, A.A. showed me wisdom to see my purpose, to strive for my Higher Power's plan.
Driving home one night I blacked out behind the wheel, plowing into a pole then a tree.
My life was spared, nobody knows how, it was to A.A. my Higher Power lead me.

The rope was tied around my neck, I cried, but couldn't step off the chair.
In sheer desperation I phoned the operator for help; thank God A.A. was there.
My life consisted of existing totally in the gutter; being insane; I wanted to die,
A.A. picked me up, brushed me off, gave me a bath, then said at the meeting you'll get coffee and pie.

Consumed by the madness of my disease, I found myself in jail when I had awakened.
By the grace of God and the help of A.A., the judge showed mercy giving me probation.
I swallowed a handful of pills and drank down a pint, trying to commit suicide.
After the hospital I was accepted by the hand of A.A.; now my Higher Power walks at my side.

I got into the ring with alcoholism for the title, during the first round I was down for the count;
A.A. showed me how I could really be a winner, with my Higher Power I can't strike out.
My spouse and I lived in two different worlds, filled with fear, hopelessness, and rejection.
Through the guidance of A.A. we learned what to fear, we have hope, we have direction.

As a child the *ism* began destroying my life, by the mid teens I was mentally blind.
A.A. came to me in a vision, offering me twenty-twenty; now with my Higher Power I can see fine.
Through A.A. I've recaptured my physical, emotional, and spiritual self, my appreciation words can't express.
The fact that A.A. reunited me with my Higher Power is the reality I cherish the best.

OBSTINACY AND THE FIRST DRINK

I can look the Sun straight in the eyes, and bathe in the warmth of its ray.
I can lounge comfortably on my porch during dusk, enjoying the breezes flowing my way.
I can smell the jasmine and clover in the air on a very humid and sticky day.
I can feel the little kid in me tingle my soul, hearing the laughter of children at play.
I can sense a pure cleanliness in my hands, whenever it is to God that I pray.
I can not even begin to count the many gifts I've received through the fellowship of A.A.
I can appreciate the beauty of a clear summer eve, seeing the stars flickering so far away.

I can have all these simple pleasures and many more, by being obstinate to that first drink today.
I can gaze at the clouds and see numerous images as they idly drift through the sky.
I can now express my happiness in lots of other ways, even, at times, by having tears in my eye.
I can be one of the team playing with my children, bursting with fun loving good energy.
I can say I love you to my spouse and really mean it, and know it will be received appreciatively.
I can hear a person's cry for help in desperation, and rush to offer a helping hand instinctively.
I can go on a nice Sunday drive with my family, up the mountain, on the plain, through the valley.
I can do the odd jobs my home needed ages ago that were collecting dust, rotting away, and turning gray.
I can have all these simple pleasures and many more by being obstinate to that first drink today.

PLANTING THE SEED

I remember my first meeting when I was encouraged to walk down the aisle.
The speaker said anyone with a desire to stay sober, come on down, get a chip, stay for awhile.
The chip represented the beginning of the struggle, from one to twenty-nine days.
The next was the thirty day chip, than the sixty day chip, to a pin after ninety days.

Receiving the yellow desire chip that night marked the start of a beautiful new life for me.
I didn't realize it then, but I honestly do now, I was dissolving the burden I had carried.

My life I thought was hopeless and useless, it was too late to
seek God's help now.
I didn't follow Him in the past, only thought of Him when I was
in trouble. He remembered me. How?

I thought I'd go along with the program for what it's worth,
since physically I'm here anyway.
To fake it one day at a time in this program, was 100% better
than my previous insanity.
I couldn't identify with the life stories I heard, no one went
through or felt like I had.
The problems they spoke of were nothing, their complaints was
the life I had wanted bad.

I remember pausing for a moment as he read how the program
works, I thought this is not for me.
I don't know about giving up all the good things I enjoyed in
the past, that was an impossibility.
Suddenly everyone rose when he said closing, and so did I; my
hands were grabbed, I wondered why.
At the end of the prayer I heard: keep coming. It was time to
say goodbye.

Now there were smiles, hugs, hand shaking, and kisses, they all
seemed programmed as far as I could see.
I wondered, do you have to be programmed to live a happy life,
to feel free in the sea of humanity?
Is there Higher Power whom I call God; what the heck is this
program all about?
I think I'll come back for just a few more meetings, I'll pay
attention, I'll really find out.

THE MIRACLE OF THE SPIRITUAL AWAKENING

I must be different or something, I don't know; I haven't seen lightening yet.
I hear of all the people who've had a spiritual awakening, maybe it's not for me to get.
I've given up all my associations with alcohol; I know that's beyond my control.
Whenever it tries to force itself into my life, it is to my Higher Power that I let it flow.
I remember there was a time when I was so insane, I can't see how I wasn't committed,
I was a complete failure every time I played god, I'd know it but just couldn't admit it.

I went to ninety meetings in ninety days, that's exactly what I was told to do.
I took the cotton out of my ears and put it in my mouth, but still no miracle.
I've always offered to help others, and I still do; every day I'm looking to do good deeds.
I try to carry the message in everything I do; when asked, I think I plant good seeds.

I work at being humble, I try to be kind, I'm apologetic when I make a mistake.
I honestly try to work the twelve steps every day; this spiritual awakening, how long does it take?
I try hard to be and stay close to God, I also ask for "wisdom" every night when I pray.

I'm vocal at asking blessings and praying for others, but for my awakening I don't know what to say.

Well, I'm not going to get huffy or loft; hey, I can always "fake it till I make it."
I'll just take it one day at a time, maybe one day me this miracle will also hit.
Wait a minute, my life today compared to how it was then, is the awakening I've wanted so desperately.
God knows how much I can carry from day to day; He has given me bit by bit all along the way.
It's amazing, all this time I've expected to be zapped because miracles descend from higher levels.
I looked for it to come gazing at mountains and boulders, when all the time I've received it through pebbles.

FACES OF HUMILITY

I'm humiliated with the fact that I'm *powerless* over alcohol.
I get so humiliated at times when my son deliberately disobeys my instructions.
Hey, did you see that, we were winning; I was so humiliated when he dropped the ball.
How could you, how dare you humiliate me before my friends and associates?
Would you believe it had taken me six hours of humiliation to move it past the wall.
You know, these stupid little rules gives me so much humiliation.
Speaking of humiliation, I sat in jail three days begging my heart out for a phone call.
That's it! I'm humiliated beyond repair; after eight times I'll never have another operation.
I'm humiliated with the fact that I'm *powerless* over alcohol.

I was so humiliated, I was standing next in line for three hours when they closed the station.
He humiliated me even more when he gave me aspirins; he well knows I need Tylenol.
You're really trying to humiliate me spitefully, because I want a separation.
Let's humiliate that drunk, he was a doctor, now look at him, let's make him crawl.
Why do you humiliate me with such trifling arguments, I wouldn't put you through that subjection.
I'm humiliated with the fact that I'm *powerless* over alcohol.
You call me a hundred times a day with these humiliating trivial situations.
I worked, saved, and scuffed for this opportunity, through humiliation blew it all.
The country of Japan was extremely humiliated after the bomb fell which brought destruction.
So what if I'm small, why humiliate me; all my life I've been told I would never be tall.
Every time I take control, it's disaster; it's through humiliation I've learned to follow my Higher Power's direction.
I'm humiliated with the fact that I'm *powerless* over alcohol.

CLASSES AND MEETINGS

Going to classes and going to A.A. meetings is all the same to me. At classes you work on a profession, at meetings you work on being a human. In classes you learn teachings, in meetings you learn suggestions.

It's the learning that remains unchanged.

In classes you seek grades, at meetings you seek aids. It's what you seek that's rearranged. In class you respect the teacher, at meetings you respect the speaker.

Respect is the key word to keep in mind.

From the classes you can reap dollars, from meetings you do reap followers.
Reap is the word to underline.
In classes you're graded by performance, at meetings you're graded by endurance. Making the grade and maintaining is your goal. In classes you trust questions, at meetings you trust suggestions.

Here trust is the word to behold.

In classes you look for opportunity, at meetings you look for community. The looking is the same in these lines. After classes your strength's in your degree, after meetings your strength's in you and me.

Strength is the enabler of all times.

Look, learn to seek respect in yourself and others, reap goodness, don't devour. Trust the strength you draw from honesty, you'll be graded by your Higher Power.

NO MISTAKES

What do you mean I made a mistake, I never made a mistake in my life.
I've been fortunate, lucky, or in the right place at the right time, don't believe me just ask my wife.
A mistake I don't make, I look before I proceed, I learned that at a very young age.
My spirit is free and was meant to be, you won't find me sitting in some cage.
Mistakes are for fools, who stray from the rules, too stupid to obey.
All they really have to do is tow the line, but no, they want to do it their way.

I realize each individual is entitled to one, although one may be
all it takes.
I'll save mine 'til the day I die, and even that probably won't be
from mistakes.
I don't stop to look back, I keep pushing ahead, I know what
just passed me by.
I keep my mind clear, I can even grab a beer, without even
blinking an eye.
Just keep it plain and eliminate the pain, that way you avoid all
the hurts.
There's enough trash to trip you up fast, leave it there for all the
crazy jerks.
I knew you were dead wrong when you said I made a mistake,
why, that's really bizarre.
If there's any more you want to know, all you have to do is say
so, I'll be down the street at the bar.

BEING MUTE AND SPEECHLESS

I'm mute, I can't talk, I lost my voice, I can't say what's on my
mind,
I lost my sound from a powerful disease, I'm truly grateful I'm
not also blind.
I get so much of a lift when I attend the meetings, inside I'm
really pleased,
I can identify with most everything I hear, my response they
can't hear from me.
I have a story to tell and I'd like to share, but who could read
my mind's tales,
I'm an alcoholic as most everyone else here, I've also hoofed
the same old trails.
I used to talk ten miles a minute, now I can't produce a word all
day,
Oh **God,** how I wish I could speak your name, when we hold
hands at the meetings and pray.

I have no need for pencil and pad at the meetings, I'd hate to
impose that way,
I've sat at some meetings with tears in my eyes, that's a price
I'll have to just pay.
I've wanted many times to aid a newcomer, to help explain how
the program really works,
I learned so much throughout the years, unable to pass it on
certainly irks.
I don't need, at this point, any special sympathy; I'm not
experiencing any regression,
I depend on being active in our A.A. group, my problem is
with my expression.
I bring my mind and body into these rooms, that's my way of
giving support,
I wish it was more I could give at the meetings, because A.A.
is my only resort.

LONELINESS

I felt loneliness as a child growing up with no friends, being
introverted I seemed shy.
I never did make friends well, not even in school, I couldn't
trust anyone to ask why.
I played by myself and even took pride in being a loner, I never
learned how to share.
I'd laugh and cry alone while no one understood me, except the
ear of my teddy bear.

I maintained the honor roll and was a good kid at home, there
was little for my parents to mention.
I did all the good things I thought everyone would like, but still
I got no attention.
While exploring the cellar I found a bottle of booze, I was
overcome with curiosity.
I took a few drinks, I felt the burning inside, I now began to
feel very silly.

As time went on I began to nip before and after school, on
weekends, holidays, and celebrations.
Regularly, I'd creep to the cellar where I hid my friend, then
I'd handle all situations and occasions.
For the next years alcohol had been faithful, it consumed my
shyness and produced superiority.
From the meekness I became a bully; at will, where the alcohol
led I followed recklessly.

I remember sitting at the bar alone yet crowded; buying rounds
and receiving false praise.
Running to the bar around two in the morning in a panic, afraid
to face the dawn of the new day.
I remember not remembering the events of the past evening, I'd
awaken again in my car alone.
There was no one in the world who would understand my
problem, no help could I get on the phone.

Seeking death, I was sidetracked into a rehab center, as in a
dream I was finally loved and had peers.
I was given the knowledge to seek and find true friendship
which is what I've longed for all these years.
Amazingly, no part of my life has ever been unique in any way,
that thought chained me to alcohol hopelessly.
Though rehab, loneliness was rejected, through A.A. friendship
is respected, now I have community.

SURRENDER

To surrender is to give up control, to be forced against one's
will;
To deliver one's hopes upon a person, place, or thing, is
certainly a bitter pill,
To cede to some other power under pressure, to entrust with no
appeal,

To relinquish one's hopes blindly through pains, to be pressed
into a bowing ordeal;
To realize one's expectations have been toppled, to feel sorrow
mixed with humility,
To have one's dreams shotgunned before one's eyes, to have
one's trust ended in adversity;
To commit one's objectives to the sandbag of defeat, to renounce
one's intentions to submission,
To deliver one's goals to heartbreaking frustration, to realize
powerlessness consumed one's ambition;
To fall short of one's desire by an unreasonable demand, to have
one's strength turned into weakness,
To be ordered to conclude, deprived of a reason, to be
compelled to cease, yielding only distress,
To be forced into submission forsaking one's direction, to make
one's aspirations keel to termination;
To be required to hold the white flag and still face annihilation,
to see one's high aim collapse to prostration;
This surrender sounds awfully strong to me, a tough force that I
dare not challenge.
If I had at my disposal all the weapons of man, still I'll mount
no threat, there'd be no balance;
To surrender seems so negative and unfair, it projects fear,
distraction, and humiliation,
Once it confronts you, you've demanded to submit, with no
questions, answers or retaliation;
To surrender to me is actually giving up an identity, whether I
wanted to or not I have no say,
I surrendered to the fact that I'm powerless over alcohol, I
surrendered to the program of A.A.
I also know I'll never surrender one hundred percent, because
that's perfection and I have a disease.
With a conscience I surrendered to my Higher Power, whose
pure perfection can be shared with me.

TRUTH'S ABOUT ME

I saw more pretty white teeth this day
Then all the ivory in the world combined.
I saw more rosy adored cheeks than ever before.

I've got more friends that really love me
Then some nations have people to rule over.
I'll honestly love this new life forever more.

I have found the fountain of true peace.
My search is over, no need stumbling anymore;
I can rest, relax, love and let it flow.

I'm added to the good number that made it.
Although others betted that I wouldn't hold on,
I don't burden myself with resentment, I let it go.

I've shed most of the old to walk with the new,
It's a relief dumping that load off my chest;
I now have the freedom I've searched for through life's paths.

I'm directly connected to a power source called A.A.,
I can recharge at will randomly,
I get the energy from my Higher Power that lasts.

TEMPTATION'S ANSWER

Recently I heard from a "dear" old friend of mine, we've been
so close for such a long time.
The key in his voice unleashed those special memories, from
the good old days, the kind that blow my mind.

He knew I had been through the rehab program, and actively
working within the steps of A.A.
He really loves the bright lights and so do I, but now our minds
don't exactly sway the same way.

We laughed and we talked about many things, hashing over
memories, out pops that old insane desire.
He's convinced he can handle it and maintain control, my
memories of my fall tells me I'm the wiser.

He dangled a proposition that ordinarily I couldn't refuse, I
thought, is this an opportunity or a test?
I could say yes and get involved, who'd know but me, I thought,
would it be carrying garbage on my chest?

It's so hard to say no when presented with a burning desire, that
you dreamed of containing for so long.
Finally after all the sacrifice, suffering, and pain, to say no is
insane, am I crazy, what's wrong?

Every thought that said yes I turned in my mind; the answers
which ended in maybe I narrowed to a no.
As the temptation inflated attempting to sweep me away, I
remembered the rehab and A.A., I let it go.

It honestly is so wonderful to side step all situations; when feeling uncomfortable, just give up control.
The wisdom to know the difference is the decision to make, when in doubt let **God,** He will let you know.

I pondered all the thoughts and most of the possibilities, the rewards would most likely fill his cup.
Next to the hope and the miracles of my High Power, I realize nothing in this world could ever add up.

I had plenty of time to make up my mind, I decided not to get involved or put my **God** on low.
I picked up the phone and got my friend on the line, I said, I appreciate the offer, but the answer is still no.

SKIPPING MEETINGS

Once I heard a person say, "I haven't been to a meeting during the past six months."
"I seeked my Higher Power every day and I prayed, I wasn't what you call out to lunch.
I was just confronted with so many persistent activities, free time was hard to find.
My Higher Power knows I'll never abandon Him or stray, that's burned in my heart and mind.
I figured I'd receive a bad time from you members, I wanted to get my activities out of the way.
I've been preparing myself for a good pouncing from you, so I stalled from day to day.
I really missed these meetings, I missed all of your faces, to me it means the years of my sobriety.
I know you've been burning candles for me, I feel I let you and myself down consciously."
A few of the other members who knew this person very well, cracked a few surface jokes.

They wanted to roll out the welcome mat and show understanding smiles, their way was with pokes.
Our discussion meeting focused entirely on this person's plight, it wasn't preset or our plan.
At the discussion meetings, we just let the topics flow, we look to identify whenever we can.
I identified strongly with this person's situation, even though in the program I was still young.
At first I thought maybe I should just sit and listen, but a true member I had truly become.
I spoke of my past problems and my weaknesses, my relationship with my **God** I felt existed;
My solutions that I felt didn't work, and how I kept stumbling, how the truths in my mind were twisted.
I spoke of the anguish I felt from lack of response, my prayers like letters blown in the wind.
Never did I receive a reply or an answer; I'd find myself facing issues alone again and again.
I spoke of how I learned sobriety isn't measured in years, it's a manner of living in **God's** protection.
Communication with Him is essential to my existence, I get it by attending the meetings for His direction.
After the hour had expired, this person's eyes had that gleam, which comes with serenity, being humble and meek.
Before our prayer this person said, "It's good to be back home, I hope to see you all back here next week."

COMMUNICATIONS WITH HIM

I grew up as a child going to church every week; in me His seed was planted at an early age.
My teachers taught me understanding which brought fear; the only way to His grace was to pay His wage.
In my early teen years I wondered why I never received a message from the many times I had prayed.
By myself I decided in essence to just run wild, I was having fun, I didn't think from Him I swayed.

As a young man I was getting in trouble with my parents and
police, I had a problem abiding by authority.
At times I'd wake up in jail with alcohol on my breath, then I'd
seek God with tears in my eye.
My tears would turn into resenting humility; oh God, how could
you desert me this way.
You know how I feel about you inside; if I could get my hands
on you, I'd make you pay.

With all the means at Your disposal, I've never received a
message, there's no way You could fail.
A letter or lightening bolt, a phone call or a sign, not even a
telegram through overnight zap mail.
For years I've wobbled now with a family of my own, I've faced
death more times than I can recall.
When I awaken in my car in front of my house in the morning;
of the night before, I only remember having a ball.

There were the times I can't remember falling asleep; waking in
a strange place days or weeks later.
I told myself it was normal, everyone I knew did it too, not
realizing I was safe by a power far greater.
I never had time to say I love you to my children, they knew it,
they could easily read my mind.
I'd always find myself being dropped into the sunshine with
them, just before convincing myself I was blind.

I gave the credit to good fortune, luck or a secret power in me,
my unconscious mind had steered me clear.
Not ever thinking it was God trying to communicate with me in
my despair through blackouts and fear.
Since my involvement in A.A., I talk to God every day, I offer
Him my thanks, gratitude and praises.
At the meeting is how He talks back to me through others, using
words, emotions, and phrases.

NON-ALCOHOLIC REWARDS

I've changed my drink from alcohol to soda, "kool-aid," iced
tea, juice, and lemonade.
The first thing I noticed almost immediately, was my amazement
with all the monies I've saved.
My total expenses from Monday to Friday actually cost me in
dollars but few.
After, eliminating the car and eliminating the house, I should
eliminate my cigarettes too.

Nowadays I take my spouse to the movies and I invite my spouse
out to dine sometime.
We could go bowling or visiting or to the amusements with the
kids, my day remains just fine.
We go to meetings together about twice a week, I'm active in
A.A., my spouse too.
My life has most definitely changed for the better, no need to
ask myself why I waited so long.

Life really hasn't changed, I feel its aches and pains, I face the
same problems as do my peers.
I diligently search for solutions as far as I can, but then to my
Higher Power I give it before giving into fears.
I seek and retrieve that special strength each morning before
starting my day, to support me in my times of weakness.
Although I know this strength and can feel its power inside me,
I'm always amazed by its shapes in my meekness.

You know, I feel like I've developed a way of turning into a
superman as I out-muscle the problems flowing my way.

Actually, for the first time in my life, loneliness has disappeared;
it has become so simple holding negativity at bay.
The garbage can I've carried inside for all too many years, has
turned into a treasure chest of good things.
I receive great enjoyment through my relationships with others,
and from the serene peace honestly brings.

Having a conscience and employing it is a gift I've received in
sobriety, which seems also a first for me.
I remember the times I boasted about not having a conscience,
not realizing without one is only insanity.
I came from existing in a near constant blackout to living in
heaven's light, thanks to the fellowship of A.A.
I know there are many paths to take in life searching for the
answers; my Higher Power chose this path, I'm glad it was
this way.

NO ELEVATORS, ONLY STEPS

I surrendered to the fact I'm powerless over alcohol, that my life
had become unmanageable at best.
My life and my dreams were set free in the basement, the
elevator was out-of-order, I had to take the steps.

I came to believe in a power greater than myself at the rehab
center, then I was blessed with my sanity next.
I was instructed to follow the program and suggestions of A.A.,
and to take my time working with the steps.

I made the decision to turn my will and life over to the care of
God as I understood Him, and everything else I had left.
This I could only do gradually by taking one day at a time, the
path is paved through the middle of the steps.

I made a searching and fearless moral inventory of myself; I
objectively reviewed memory, putting myself to the test.
I enlisted to side with honesty and truth as my guide, the three
of us promptly headed straight to the steps.

I've admitted to *God,* myself, and another human being the
exact nature of my wrongs, which I did in depth.
Afterward I felt like running, all I could think of was to get away
fast, but I found comfort walking in the steps.

I'm entirely ready to have *God* remove all my defects of
character, I would like to take that weight off my chest.
It's really been a burden to carry throughout all the years, I
found a disposal as I climbed the steps.

I humbly asked Him to remove my shortcomings, I know I have
them along with many regrets.
Since these imperfections can be taken from me, I pray they
will; I'll put them on the elevator, I'll take the steps.

I made a list of all people I have harmed, and I'm willing to
make amends to them all, I'll be honest.
There are those situations when I'll have to wait for the proper
moment, until then I'll rehearse with the steps.

I'm constantly making direct amends to people, I've harmed
whenever possible, except when to do so would hurt them
or others.
I excel when I humble myself, it feels good to say I'm sorry, for
so many years it had pushed me in the gutters.

I continue to take personal inventory and when I'm wrong, I
promptly admit it; this is a habit I seem to enjoy.
I'm always striving to be near the perfection A.A. is based, my
Higher Power's will and strength I employ.

I seek, through prayer and meditation to improve my conscious
contact with my *God* and for knowledge of His will for me.
I also pray for the power to carry that out; I know whatever
strength I'll need will be found within A.A.

I had a spiritual awakening resulting from these steps; I try to carry the message to alcoholics, practicing these principals in my affairs.
There were many occasions when I though it would be easier to take the elevator, but my Higher Power lead me to the stepping stairs.

YESTERDAY'S DREAMS

Yesterday I dreamed I was surrounded by love, offered to me freely with no price to pay.
I was one among many and the many were for one, I was part of this strange community.
In this dream my will had a freedom of choice, there wasn't force, restrictions, or obligations.
I could also choose to remain as I was if I wanted, there were no rules ordering transformations.

I received knowledge, wisdom and was offered direction, a map of understanding was given to me.
When traveling, if I became lost, I only had to press a button, I'd be connected with help immediately.
In the dream people didn't have many problems at all, the one who did I couldn't tell from the rest.
It seemed that the garbage carried inside didn't hold with them, they weren't bogged with it on their chest.

They seemed happy most times which struck me a bit odd, especially when I saw the men embracing themselves.
They had that look of awareness, a mirror in their eyes, of life; they seemed to have come from all levels.
In the dream when one person spoke, the others earnestly listened, sincerity and concern was very apparent.
If one person had a troublesome problem on their mind, the others would share suggestions until its descent.

In reality, no one could possibly be as happy as they seemed,
but I must admit, I felt euphoric seeing their smiles.
There seemed an interaction among them that was truly
irresistible; to experience that I'd walk days and miles.
I thought if life could really be enjoyed in the real world, that
living a fully happy life would be a breeze.
At least I have my dreams to use as an escape from the hell I
live, because this world is so damned hard to please.

As far as I can recall, I've always dreamed these crazy dreams;
I've dreamed I had hundreds of real friends.
I can still remember communicating with a Higher Power in the
dreams, regretfully once I wake, it all ends.
The fact is this is the only life I have to work with for
happiness, if I choose to sit and wait, it will pass me by.
I wish I knew of a place where I could go and just dream,
because there are times I feel I want to die.

HEAVENLY LINGO

At my recent alumni reunion a fact revealed itself to me in a
vision.
It had appeared to me upon arrival, the feeling was definitely
intuition.
I realized the level of communication of which I was about to
take part,
Was a lively, unknown to words of description, this shop talk
was from the heart.
The happiness in the air was so thick it could have been sliced
with a knife.
The dreamlike environment was serene; the euphoria brilliant
and so very nicc.
Shared in the honest eye contact with my counselors, friends,
and peers.

Although the words couldn't fall from our lips, our eyes spoke through to our ears.
The strong, firm, tender, loving grip of our hands sent messages to our brains,
We all fight the same deadly disease every day, but none showed any sign of strain.
That strong reassuring embrace is so marvelous, its presence removes all fears away.
Our smiles tell us our love is mutual as our emotions soar the heights of our ecstasy.
Warm soft kiss electrifies our cheeks sending jubilant thoughts glowing in our mind.
Our pliable tone of voice wraps truth and wisdom around meaning rendering it refined.
These are some examples of the way we can communicate and send messages to and fro.
To actually hold a conversation at this level is what I call—true heavenly lingo.
As I scan the previous few months of my life, the visionary pieces now materialize.
There were those days since my involvement with A.A. when I experienced that natural high.
I feel it is a blessing to be enjoyed from my Higher Power—nutrition for my spiritual health,
Just to be a part of the group speaking from the heart, to me is like visiting heaven itself.

ASSOCIATIONS

As I gaze through my chronicle of associations in life, very few faces can I really see.
The images are vague, distant, and unnaturally remote, only one or two do I see clearly.
My associations were myself with the dreams of my mind as I stumbled through life, from boundary to border.

Blindness was my choice; help was unknown to my voice, I was
like a child which grew no older.
I never progressed to step two nor landed on any other, my
desire was out taking a swim.
To nothing I would cling, after passing away everything, with
empty hands my desire would go swim again.
Union was not for me, leave friendship to destroy, mingle, and
rejoice with procrastination.
No problem, I would progress, when the time comes I would
think best, I would climb, void of hesitation.
I will be the one to rule with the iron in my fists, sharing my
love with my throne.
When I turn old and gray, I'll look back regretfully, and wonder
why inside I feel so alone.

HUMILITY

Humility is a gift I've received through my Higher Power, one
of the gifts from birth I've used.
I've always associated it with pain, hurt, and misunderstanding,
and being abused.

From humility, I would run and avoid at all costs with it I did
not want to deal.
Every time in my life that I've been forced to acknowledge it,
my laughter it would usually steal.

I felt humility, because no matter how hard I had tried, still I
could not gain the control.
Through frustration and aggravation and other negative
reactions, I was totally unable to grow.

To me, humility is to have a desire of certain accomplishments,
and have the means to bring about the ends.
No matter how much you try to contain, the results stay the
same; finishing in defeat again, again, and again.

Humility can produce rage, that burning fire inside your eyes,
the kind that melts rocks before you can stumble.
It wasn't until through the teaching of A.A. that I realized that
true humility can equal simply being humble.

TIME-LESS

I lack motivation and embrace procrastination, I'm always last
or late.
I can sit and watch the clock or wind my watch, something
always tells me to wait.
I can plan a trip weeks or months in advance, and won't
remember until the next day.
I can spend days on end writing a speech, by the time I deliver
it, who would know what I had to say.

I usually stall until the last minute out of habit, rarely do I spark
myself in time.
I'm so sluggish that even time always flies, I'd be the last to
know if I were blind.
Sometime I'm so slow, my shadow leaves me behind, that's
really a shame I admit.
When I assure myself that I'll do better, on the very next
occasion again, I forget.

When my family and I prepare to go out for a ride, they're in
the car while I'm still preparing to leave.
I'd swat at all insects flying in my vicinity, until I got stung in
the head by a bee.
I was sent a draft notice two weeks ahead, I arrived after 2 p.m.
or over seven hours late.
I never knew I could pick myself up from the gutter, for years I
laid there thinking it was my fate.

I thought I could drink while driving and maintain control, until
a tree stepped into my path.
She said don't jump in the pool, the water's been drained, after
drinking I did and fell on my ass.
The Governor said if you're caught with a gun, you're going to
jail, I did and the judge put me away.
I bought more sale items then I had money in the bank, I
became upset the check bounced on the eighth day.

A.A. won't kill you, but alcohol surely will, it's a proven fact;
with A.A., I'll be the last to see.
Living life without a drink seems horrible to me, I'll try it
though I know I'd probably hate sobriety.
I remember the saying, association brings simulation, I'll go to
the meetings, but I won't accept their schooling.
Hey, this is a switch, maybe it's time I give myself some time,
after all, in the end who am I fooling?

ARGUMENTS

Sometimes I argue with my spouse, through heated aggravation
to the point of separation.
How could we have grown so different through the years?
Like a child I'd pout, as if deaf I would shout, revenge engulfs
my imagination.
I wonder, why should I have to feel so bad and end up shedding
the tears.
The love I have for my spouse runneth over my cup, it's
beautiful, comfortable and protecting.
That's the intensity of which I like to express my feelings
constantly.
Why can't we maintain that high level, why does it fade,
dwindle and keep regressing?
Why we can't dwell on that level and share; that is really
baffling to me.

Once reaching frustration, I become very spiteful, for me arguments import negative feelings inside.
I feel compelled to inject more pain than I felt in an attempt to justify.
I find myself searching for some unique weapon to use which will give me the upper hand in stride,
To make the knees of my spouse bend before me and at my mercy.
After all, that's exactly what was done to me, all I want to do is strike back and get even.
If I can't win, I'll never be happy in a one-sided relation.
I'll break up or end everything in divorce, I'll offer no sympathy, compassion or reason.
I'll move on in search of happiness, I'll put my all in a new situation.
That's when the thought struck me that separation is not an answer, only a falsified illusion.
Arguments are a part of life, it actually doesn't matter with who.
If I'm really willing to offer someone all my love, understanding and compassion.
Then who in the world can be a better candidate I know than you.

EGO OR PRIDE

On a Tuesday morning I started a new job, installing equipment on a construction site.
The job is very tedious and constantly on the move, I can handle it, I'm fit, I'll be all right.
I stood on top of a step ladder unsupported, trying to maintain balance while reaching to the sky.
Using every bone and muscle in my body, while chips of metal and dirt fell into my eye.

Everyone knew this job paid very good wages, but when I started a slip read four dollars an hour.
I really don't mind beginning at the bottom, I wouldn't give my ego or pride that power.
I was told by the foreman that I'd see the manager on Thursday, at which time we'd discuss my pay.
For eight hours I climbed up and down the ladder, without any breaks along the way.

After I got home I tired very quickly, when I looked at my bed my energy faded away.
When I opened my eyes I realized I missed my meeting, it was six a.m., time to start a new day.
At the job it was back to the ladder, by midday I noticed the aches and pains begin to set in.
But still I was determined to give it my all, as I felt the pains from strains I'd smother it with a grin.

That evening my sponsor called me on the telephone, I shared the new challenge I had in my life.
I didn't go into detail to avoid my ego or pride, besides with my job situation, I had no real strife.
I got band-aids from my wife for my raw fingers, in a hot bath with epsom salts I soaked.
The aches and pains now engulfed my whole body, still I wouldn't let my ego or pride take note.

Thursday morning I completed the bracing of over 11,000 units, the manager I never did get to see.
For the rest of the day I lifted and placed heavy equipment, it was obvious the foreman lied to me.
Friday I was told I must work thirteen hours a day, at four dollars an hour from Monday to Thursday.
I told the foreman I have other important activities in my life, especially when it comes to my sobriety.

I was determined not to allow my ego or pride to stand in the way, I was determined not to quit no matter what.
When it comes to my sacrificing my A.A. involvement and the people, there's no ifs, ands or buts.

GARBAGE

For many years I hoarded the refuse of life, thinking that one
day it may turn to gold.
The dregs of my tears were used as fuel for my fears, making
life's truths even harder to behold.
The rubble at my feet began to hinder my step, on my socks
and cuffs it would cling.
The filth began to weigh heavily upon my ankles, gliding
through the air it would wave and sing.
The sewage made headway, climbing up my leg; I disregarded it
because sewage doesn't flow up hill.
The slop I knew was useful for feeding pigs, but the knit fabric
of my trousers it began to fill.
The debris blanketed the area of my pant legs, the dreck acting
like glue held the debris in place.
Then the dust camouflaged the entire garment, the garbage had
now spread totally about my waist.
The kelter progressed continually up my shirt tail, replacing the
bright colors with dingy and gray.
The junk had taken hold of the belt I was wearing, all too soon
it would give way to decay.
The litter I didn't discard I put in my shirt pocket, it's funny but
I was waiting to deposit it in a garbage can.
The muck had clearly gained the control of my collar, with my
head in a noose I reached for a helping hand.
To the rehabilitation center that hand had led me, confusion was
all with which I could identify.
I was taken out of my shoes to eliminate the source of my
problems, I was told to expel the whys.
I was shown more beautiful new garments then I ever imagined,
as my belt and trousers fell to the floor.

I began to appreciate how well everyone there dressed, tossing my shirt in my pile near the door.
I showered with hope, love, kindness, and understanding, I dined with truth and real honesty.
I was clad in the garments of my choosing, they were woven in comfort, peace and serenity.
I was given a shield to fend off future garbage, I call it my Higher Power associated with A.A.
I know if it wasn't for Marworth Rehab Center, with that noose, I'd probably be dead today.

TO THE TEST

I had my first taste of alcohol sipping from beer as a child.
The taste on my tongue was different, so I stood testing for a while.
As I swallowed, I felt bits of panic which were smothered by my Dad's smile.
The warmth surged inside me, alcohol was present, there was no denial.
I've tested the waters learning how to swim, I test my strength at times.
I've tested my nerves being foolish with friends, I've tested my patience standing in lines.
I've tested my ignorance acting selfishly, I tested my parents to see how far I could go.
I've tested my willpower over alcohol to no avail, I've tested the depths of my sorrow.
I've tested the foods of many nations, I test the honesty I know I possess.
I've tested the laws by which we live, I test the heart inside my chcst.
I've tested living life in the fast lane, I've tested danger in my hand.

I've tested frustration many times in the past, I test the lies of man.
I've tested the knowledge I've gained from books, I test the best of my ability.
I've tested the appreciation I've seen in others, I've tested man's true humanity.
I've tested the reasons for doing good deeds, I've tested the taste of tears.
I've tested loneliness in all its glory, I test the memories I hold so dear.
All the things that I've tested throughout the years, seeking answers to many questions.
Chasing clues that ended down one-way streets, offering no solutions or suggestions.
Well, I've tested the rehab, I've tested my Higher Power, and I've tasted the power of A.A.
I put myself to the test for honesty, as I flow through the twelve steps every day.

KINDNESS

When I do a good deed, I plant a good seed;
Oh how it fulfills me so to see and know I can grow.
The glow I feel inside, I'll use for my pride.
My power source is timeless, I'll engulf you in kindness.

Kindness is that love, special from high above.
Having had held the gift, I pass it on.
The sparkle I feel inside, the pats from my guide,
The glow that glistens in my eye, makes impossible to lie.

I had to first understand, to offer a helping hand.
Tumbling in the blindness, I arose with kindness.
I couldn't utter yes yesterday, today a new vocabulary.
Good fortune fell on me, here take it.

The dirt is but a dream, I've joined the other team.
To inner strength and power, I'll stand as a flower.
With kindness I soar aloft, exempt; bark, scream or balk.
I seek the faith of an ant, like a rock to be tolerant.

Kindness is a lock made for no key.
Like the wind I'm handled gently,
Whose security I can cloak indefinitely;
Mentally I'll get plenty to grow simply.

SOBRIETY

Shortly after I had awakened this morning on this average day,
Somewhere between my first cup of coffee and being blinded by the sun's ray,
As I peacefully pondered through my memory, preparing to arrange my day,
To my surprise I suddenly realized, that I was really, truly happy.

Wait a minute, I paused, could it really be this easy, or just my imagination?
Feeling this good without any effort—there must be an explanation.
Is this what I was told would happen? Am I having a flashback in disguise?
As the warmth of the gleam flushed in my eye, my thought said, keep it simple stupid, eliminate the whys.

A broad smile spread across my face, like a child I felt the surging glee.
Laughter seemed to have sprung from my every pore, what in the world is happening to me.
My vision grew sharply, bright and tingly, the word "dream" flashed through my mind.
I felt so awesomely elated, my Higher Power has really been kind.

For so long have I longed for a sensation. I never even imagined could be this great.
Insane, I had been stumbling in the wrong direction, allowing my disease to dictate.
I feel like shouting to the world, or putting out a communique, or renting a billboard sign.
To say A.A. has a very effective answer for keeping one's heart and mind aligned.

I felt fulfilled as I inhaled deeply, when abruptly the fact revealed itself to me.
The sensation I was experiencing was a level of life that I could choose to roam to daily.
Oh now I know why I feel happy, now I know why I feel so free,
Because after I opened by eyes this morning, my first thoughts were of my sobriety.

FEAR

Fear is directly represented by the state of the unknown in association with the unforeseen future.
Its conception actually begins in the mind of its victim, one's imagination is used as a lure.
It feeds on negative predictions, expectations, possibilities, hopes, presumptions, and intentions.
Along with the I thoughts, I figure, I feel, I know, I sense, I guess, and the superstitions.

Fear is such a powerful frightening emotion, its face alone could shock and stop your heart.
Fear can terrify you and force you to look the other way appallingly as it tears your logic apart,

Fear is the one tool that should never be left uncontained when difficulties are present or pressing.
Fear has at its disposal an abundance of disguises which make it unrecognizable and keep you guessing.

Fear can appear within the blink of an eye without sound, pounding your heart in your chest.
Fear can propel you through the heights of insanity as it dangles you before the teeth of death.
Fear like a chameleon can shed its colors and can turn from gruesome to appear like innocence.
Fear will move into your life with bag and baggage, and irrelevantly demand you pay to it rent.

Fear maintains a black hole full of illusions and delusion, for the purpose of destroying its prey.
Fear will take a healthy, clean, beautiful specimen of life and turn it into ghastly decay.
Fear can rob your voice, speech, motivation, and will and leave you standing with cold feet.
Fear will scare you into severe hairsplitting nervousness, and dare you to leave the edge of your seat.

Some fears can be beneficial for guiding ones life, keeping one from being prey to the outer-bound.
Some fears are aids to maintain one in good health, and to keep one from falling upon the ground.
Some fears are gifts from our Higher Power, raising and exhalting us to tower over difficulty.
Some fears you develop as you travel through the day like the one I have of life without A.A.

MOTIVATOR

I had entirely overlooked the possibility of my writings as being a gift.

I considered it as an art or a profession employed by the
movements of my wrist.
I remember when I was in the fifth grade, I had written a piece
about the wind.
My teacher presented me with the class award, which made me
so happy then.
Since then I found relaxation dabbling through the years, the
phrases forming in my mind.
I would excel when in jail or hospitalized, when my dreams I
had time to seriously define.
Looking back, I could see my burning curiosity for words in my
intense search for their meanings.
Even though I was unable to use most of the words in my daily
life, I still found them fascinating.
I can relate now to my love of the dictionary and how that love
in me never faded away.
For approximately twenty-three years I've had an affair with
words, just as I do today.
I've written novels, biographies, and hundreds of songs and
poems through the years.
I've written countless letters for others to their lovers, that even
from me brought tears.
Somewhere in my foggy past, I remember hearing someone say
in casual conversation:
". . . that professional writing was the field of impossible
penetration," that robbed my motivation.
Hence I'd only write as a hobby whenever I found the idle time
to record an inspiring vision.
Fortunately in my life, I've had plenty idle time from always
recuperating after a collision.
But now my relationship with A.A. has reunited me with *God,*
my Higher Power, my dream.
My writings are merely letters to Him with hope He may know
it is my utter being I'm offering.
My words are all I have to give and words can be mightier than
a sword, that's no trick.
I still have my dictionary, my love, my words, and my spirit,
also my motivation.

Thank you Nick.

NEGLECT

I neglected my better judgment in my early youth, through my
curiosity I was left throttled.
Helplessly I watched as my manners and respect failed; yet, in
my hand I held onto the bottle.
My very first neglect was neglecting myself, "submission,"
alcohol controlled my mind;
There were periods when I held onto the wheel, "intermission,"
but like a map I followed the line.

I neglected common sense along with the signs, I neglected
asking questions of others.
I neglected the presence of truth and honesty, I neglected when
my stomach had the flutters.
I neglected my *God* with deep sorrow and tears, I neglected my
faith in *His* works and direction.
I neglected the love and advice of my parents, I neglected the
comfort of a real home's protection.
As a young man I thought neglect had become my strength, this
strength's energy was based in alcohol.
On this strength I would lean, being profane and mean, but that
strength as I fall was of no use to me at all.

I couldn't see neglect for what it really was, I was too busy
being busy about doing nothing.
Long ago I had neglected my conscious, "what's wrong?" I
took comfort not being active in anything.
I neglected reality, I became a partner in marriage, I neglected
my spouse for alcohol and the street.
I neglected my children, I couldn't find the time, I neglected, in
times of grief, to even weep.

I neglected my work, I neglected my job, I neglected the rules and laws of this society.
I neglected the consequences, I neglected the power, I neglected to bow or accept any authority.
I had neglected that the root cause of my emptiness was directly connected to alcohol, the disease.
I had neglected to do anything about anything, until I couldn't help but notice I had no skin left on my knees.
If I neglect the fact of my spiritual awakening, or the miracle of which I embrace and dwell in every day;
Should I fall from neglect to the depths of an insane death, it would be because I didn't accept the hand of A.A.

LEARNING

I learned many things at the rehabilitation center; the ways and means of traveling through life,
Which tools to use in the vast array of situations, and in which direction to walk when I see strife.
I learned I must hold a true conscience first of all, to communicate with my Higher Power through others.
He doesn't speak directly to me, but does with others at our A.A. meetings, we're not in the gutters.

I learned honesty is a precious tool to be carried with me daily, it buys all the non-material things.
Emotionally and spiritually you'll find your many gifts, they're some of the rewards honesty brings.
I learned some of the many different meanings in life, I never cared to examine in the past.
I never figured in my life I would ever need the answers, I had become content to sit watching them pass,

I learned humility was not a negative emotion, it's one of the roads leading to comfort and shelter.
It was through humility that I've been able to arrest my disease, my life certainly has changed for the better.
I learned to ask questions when I'm in doubt and I learned I must trust other people sometime.
I learned the nice feeling of helping others, looking for no reward; I learned how easy it is to be kind.

I learned to appreciate the goodness of mother nature; I learned to view life with an objective eye.
I learned as people we must depend on one another; I learned I have a natural need at times to cry.
I learned the power of my Higher Power through the fellowship of A.A., I'm lifted by His strengthening understanding.
In my life I could see that a miracle has taken place, it was not of my doing, intention or planning.

I've learned from many experiences and paid many prices, I know I've been fortunate, there's no doubt in my mind.
Along with learning, I always receive a certain answer, it's how I heed it that will be tested in time.
I see that all the many beautiful things I've learned at rehab, and the gifts I've received to aid me in this life.
As compared to life in A.A., working the steps every day in reality, by comparison, the rehab was only a trife.

YOUR STORY

There are only three types of stories that can be told, all three are the facts on how you fell.
One is the story you prepare to tell, two is the story you tell, three is the story you forgot to tell.
I joined a speaker group after entering A.A., attending the meetings is the height of my day.

I don't work A.A. around my life, but I get a delightful charge out of working my life around A.A.
Being a part of a speakers group is good if you have a story to tell; for a newcomer, it may pave the way.
Telling your story to the group is taking a load off your chest; just open your mouth, your heart knows what to say.
I remember the first time I ever honestly attempted to tell my story, I thought it would be a piece of cake.
What I did was tell a war story with all the minute details, boy did that turn out to be a mistake.
My progression was unclear and I omitted my feelings; maybe I felt the group could read my mind.
After all the words I put into that blur I called a story, it ran thirty minutes past our dinner time.
The second time I told my story, it was after my ninety days; at an A.A. meeting I had the whole hour.
That night I realized the three types of stories; what pulled me through was honesty and my Higher Power.
I felt good-bad, plus-minus, happy-sad in a mixture of combinations, while they were shaking my hand.
The bottom line was it was accepted and they identified, that's when the three types of stories I began to understand,
The third time I told my story, it was by complete surprise, so I just opened my mouth and let it flow.
The results were comforting. I spoke on many points; I was reminded of how it gets better as you go.
The fourth time was the very next night before the group I had joined, I didn't say no, I told my story.
Our speakers had gotten lost trying to get to our meeting, I didn't say what I wanted to so I thought it was corny.
Afterwards, my sponsor told me "you did a nice job being unprepared and all, there's no reason you should worry,
because in A.A. all that's asked is that you do the best you can, and after all, you only have your story."

FAMILY AFFAIR

When I think of all the hurt and suffering I've inflicted, it brings
tears to my eyes.
I now see that I've tortured her for more than thirteen years,
insanity wore me as a disguise.
The mental anguish I've forced her to bear was undeserved, her
nerves I've held at ends.
I never had the slightest notion of my wrongs from within, as I
plowed into destruction and sin.

She must have seen what I felt inside, but could not show,
somehow she stuck with me like glue.
She struggled through my adversities besides her own; the
problems never stopped, only grew.
She continued to love me when I couldn't begin to love myself,
when in loneliness I'd go crawl and hide.
She prepared my dinner, washed my clothing and maintained
our home, while I used guilt for my pride.

My children never had a father, only a big kid named the old
man, very irresponsible and a little nuts.
They couldn't get an honest answer, ask any questions; my only
responses were ifs, ands, or buts.
My actions told them to go stand in a corner and grow for six
months, be good, I'll bring you candy and cake.
With tears I remember I never individually told them I love
them; on my part, a huge mistake.

We would go out on family drives maybe once or twice a year;
that's only if the ism said it was o.k.

I would stop at the bar to hang out with my many friends, no rush to get home it's payday.
I didn't know I was becoming known by the kids as the town drunk, and then again, I didn't care.
All I wanted was to drink my drink and mind my own business, forced involvement was very unfair.

Now that my brain can breathe again, hope has re-entered my life, the world seems new and inviting.
As long as I love myself today, I can share my love with others, the possibilities are all exciting.
I owe my family all of my deepest considerations and support, I owe my wife happiness and peace.
I owe myself true honesty and sharing with others, I owe my Higher Power my thanks for riding the beast.

NEGATIVISM

There is a positive and negative existence in every situation I face.
One must give way to the stronger power, the choice is mine in either case.
Negativity to me is gloom, doom, gray and cloudy; it equals hurt, pain and submission.
I find I'm completely swept off my feet by the negative, when I feed on superstition.
If I base my thoughts in a negative environment, I'll find only the negatives and no truths.
If I plant my tree in negative soil to grow, I can only reap negative fruits.
Negativity I once held and hoarded as if gold; its value were measured in my peril.

If I were to begin my day on a negative note, by evening it would end in disaster.
I've learned when I'm in a negative state of mind, I'm robbed of my feeling good laughter.
Negativism is a very aggressive dominating force, its growth cannot be contained.
I've seen otherwise good people brought to their knees, their behavior becomes definitely insane.
Negativity exists predominantly in the unknown, it evolves around weakness and fears.
Like a bully it pushes me around at its will, after all, it's been practiced for thousands of years.
The negative can take my sight, rendering me blind, making it impossible to see past the fog.
Once pain shocks me into breaking out or escaping, the roads all lead to being stalled or bogged.
I could be having a needed discussion with my spouse, being negative will end in argument.
When I realize I've wallowed in the anger and frustration, I too find my mental frame had been bent.
Negativity will stumble me aimlessly, going nowhere; I can fall on my face or crash into a wall.
With A.A., I can outmaneuver most all my negativities by simply remaining negative to alcohol.

MARWORTH II

This reunion is merely physical, because in my mind we're together every day.
No matter where my travels take me, I always bring along my memory.
For so many years my mind had laid dormant, I never thought to wonder why.
From sharing this miraculous program with me, my mind's limits are high in the sky.

Sharing with you is like a fantasy come true, it was here we
learned life's meaning together.
A little shaky at first I was afraid to leave, but really life with
A.A. only gets better.
Today I have the stars the moon and the sun, I romp in the snow
on the mountain top.
I've developed an attraction for Mother Nature, her revelations
to me I hope never stop.
This reunion represents two very good years of forming real
people out of broken pieces,
Saved from death, destruction, and illness, whose lives have
new meanings and leases.
I stumbled in through these doors of Marworth, my expectations
were totally unknown,
I had lost my belief in miracles and God, in pursuit of life I was
not prone.
I never thought I could enjoy life sober, I never imagined with
God I could make amends.
I never felt I'd ever really have a conscience, I never dreamed I
could have so many friends.
The fact that I was being controlled by a disease never
materialized in my mind.
With God and A.A. in my life every day, my life will shine till
the end of my time.
I'm so happy to be here with you physically, it's so beautiful
seeing the smiles on your face.
It feels great to stand, to shake your hand, to have the strength
to return your embrace.
It was here I received my desire and thirty-day chips, I'll get
my sixty-day and my pin while I'm here.
It is here at Marworth that my life recommenced, my true
gratitude will out last the years.

OUR REUNION

Just being present at our alumni reunion was like spending a day
in heaven.
Everything seemed so beautiful and serene, everyone seemed so
reverend.
There was a natural high floating about in the air which took us
all by storm.
The breeze flowed softly and rewardingly, the sun shined
brightly, the rays warm.

Welcome was stamped plainly in every heart, like a diamond,
love flickered through our eyes.
We, the winners, come to gather as one; how it really works we
can testify.
The tears of joy reflected our true blissfulness, the hugs more
than sincere.
A kiss was only an expression of speechlessness, the message
was really a soothing song to the ear.

Sobriety stood with us in all its glory, belonging to no one
person, but we all could share.
Although able to recall the dangers that made us fall, its in our
sobriety we chose to care.
Nature's fragrances mingled with us like a friendly pet,
butterflies fluttered shoulder to shoulder.
Some faces haven't been seen in the last few years, but you
know, they keep looking younger instead of older.

Beneath my feet felt like nothing was there, maybe it was a
cloud upon which we stood.

With my Higher Power in my life nothing is impossible, I would fly if He willed I should.
It seemed as if we were experiencing a dream, each of us at the exact same time.
It's as if we all were taking part in a miracle, the thoughts even now still blows my mind.

Beautiful, wonderful, and heavenly are modest words to use defining our reunion.
The words haven't been invented yet that can describe the feelings in our communion.
Oh so very fortunate we are to have each other; it's our memories I treasure as so dear.
I do look forward to seeing you every day, but if not, I'll meet you at our reunion next year.

TODAY

THE STATUE OF LIBERTY

Our Father who are in Heaven, please accept my humble praise
to Thee.
I thank you for this wonderful land, I thank you for the Statue
of Liberty.
I came to this country with merely a hope and a prayer, for I
knew not what to expect.
True freedom was my dream that flickered deep within, my
memory will never let me forget.
For me the Statue of Liberty means Philadelphia, in her eyes I
can see Washington, D.C.
Her presence was admired long before 1892, she is the binding
of America's great history.
She is the pedestal upon which dreams are made and held, she
is the conscious of our government.
She is our marker for the world to behold, yes indeed, she truly
had to be heaven sent.
Her song is carried throughout this land by riding the wind, the
meaning is found in her very name.
She is the symbol of the fiber that I'm made of, I pray God may
forever secure her flame.
She discarded the mental bonds which had held me, I found her
light while lost in humanity.
I trembled with fear of the unknown when she grasped my hand,
from the darkness she set me free.
The tears gathering in my eyes are of happiness, the warmth
racing inside effects my every pore.
The goose pimples on my arms and neck are from my gratitude,
my love for her will last forevermore.
Every time I think of these United States of America, I think
too of our great democracy.

Here along with citizenship, one inherits the right to vote in this beautiful land of the free.
Each July I celebrate my independence along with this nation, I enjoy the bombs bursting in the air.
The blues, the reds, the silvers, and the quaking of my soul, the twinkle in my eye against the glare.
I'm proud to be an American, a fact I can never deny, I can feel the pride swell inside me.
I can remember my heart a flutter in the distance in the fog, my eyes sighted the flame of Lady Liberty.

ETHIOPIA

I had fallen to the ground, I was too weak to stand; my frail
form and shattered knees could move no more.
My tears had long dried up and away, my howl was but a
whisper in pursuit of life I was losing the war.

My every exhale produced a very small burst of dust, my bulged
eyes gazed unblinking upon the earth; starvation had overtaken
me, its painful grip ripped my insides.
I thought, surely, death could be no worse.

Through all my agony and pain I managed to smile mentally, I
recalled the happy times of my yesterdays.
I enjoyed serenity as my reality drifted away a few moments,
until again I felt the sun's burning hot rays.

My tongue was void of moisture to soothe my dry cracked lips,
my heart sputtered as if this breath was my last.
I felt my energy ooze out of me, my will was losing control,
just to think became a labored task.

I moaned, oh God, please come and take my bankrupt soul.
Relieve me from this burden to which I'm tied.
What was the point of suffering? The reason was beyond my
rationale, of this life I lost face and my pride.

I thought of my wife and child who were depending on my
return for food, thus my last emotion would be grief.
Out of my numbness protruded sorrow that I welcomed openly,
I responded by tightly gritting my teeth.

With my ear pressed against the terrain since my falling, and
being at the very edge of life ready to expire, I heard the roar of
an engine in the distance.
Suddenly hope sparked in my heart igniting my fire.
Yet still I was unable to move to send out a life signal.
I fought to remain calm and retain my sanity.
An angel from heaven had to have guided this vehicle to where I
lay, for it was help and they rescued me.

Fresh air was pumped into me through a machine.
As I was tenderly rolled over onto my back.
The huddle of their bodies produced a desired shade, I was in
shock not knowing how I should react.

I was still too weak to speak or even thank them.
Once aboard their vehicle I thought only of Utopia.
While resting I saw many sacks of food, grain, and medicine,
Stamped USA-Aid from the people of Ethiopia.

DR. MARTIN LUTHER KING

Once there was a man who walked throughout this land; with
the love he felt deep in his heart exalted in his extended
hand.
He spoke of a great peace, and sang of an inspirational justice
to say the very least;
His lyrics composed the words written on the heart, of which
we all understand.

The bells of freedom he did ring, as repeatedly he'd sourge to
yank its mighty string;
As if he needed an defense he would cry, "The Constitution says
that I can."
Truth and honesty dominated his very tongue, faith continued to
move him since step one;
Truly a gem for us all to behold, was the god-like qualities
reflecting in this man.

Violence and danger did not hide, yet they fell helpless against
his stride;
Fear and intimidation combined could not sway the foundation
of his stand.
Through all the tears, pains, and jails to retreat was never one
of his qualls;
He followed that path mapped in our dreams, no power on earth
could alter that plan.

He was a multiple man of many colors, he labored for all his
sisters and brothers;
I did identify with my shade; but we all are part of this human
clan.
From his mouth the words would roll, electricity igniting the
core of my soul;
The souls of many nations he held aloft that for years had been
buried in sand.

He certainly is a blessing in disguise, I can enjoy the warm flush
of the pride in my eyes;
Yes, indeed, of he mine eyes did see, that he was born of a
seemingly unearthly brand.
Dr. Martin Luther King it is to you that I sing, from the earth to
the Heavens through everything;
Today, I still shine bright with your dream, oh thank you, thank
you, for being ever so grand.

"AMERICA'S GREATEST LADY"

America has never had a finer representative, so gracious, so
fashionable, and so debonair:
Majestically inclined by nature so she reigns, she champions
our nation with profound flair.
Elegance is the base of her makeup, she employs an allegiance
that spans years times her age;
Righteousness is found clinging upon every word she speaks,
merely an element of her heritage.
Indefatigable is her quest for justice and the American way,
unblemished are the works by her hand;
Cautiously she embarks when engaging the emotions of others,
thus defeating the visage of contraband.
Artistically she maneuvers on all planes of society, being very
receptive to those suffering and in poverty;
Straightforwardness is her approach to the plagues of this land,
thus she battles for our God given legacy.

Gallantry is hers to possess and mold as she will, courteousness
is vapored in her every expression;
Renowned are her many strides in the names of humanity,
selfishness in her, is just out of the question.
Eagerly she rises to the occasion through many organizations, to
combat sickness, disease, and ill health;
Alcoholism's epidemic has been seized by her sharp attention;
her works are more valuable than wealth.
Theaters, museums, and all the cultural and liberal arts, benefit
from the vast awareness she brings;
Education, civil rights, child abuse, and other groups reap the
positive fruits of her labors and reasonings.

Secured is her faith in her people, in her land, which her hopes, dreams, and loves are bestowed;
To the magnitude of people whose hearts she has revitalized, her mere concern lifted their heavy load.

Lofty are the affections that appear through the glare in her eyes as they reflect the sunshine of her soul;
Attestation of her walk is held exalted in her wake, her energy and enthusiasm seem exempt of toll.
Democracy has been honored with her presence and commitment, her breed is of a very special clan;
Yes, I truly admire this lady and to her I lodge my praise; please accept my thank you, Mrs. Nancy Reagan.

"BIG BROTHERS AND SISTERS"

The Big Brothers and Sisters organizers in our town, is part of a national organization;
They help the disadvantaged, the unfortunate, and lonely children, less any discrimination.
They offer our youth some special time and consideration, with real personalized attention;
They voluntarily offer their services and livelihood to the children, in warm loving affection.
They provide our children with knowledge not taught in school, dealing in humane education;
They display to the kids that being a human being comes from the heart, without specialization.
They present our children a variety of opportunities, to give them a sense of direction;
They aid the families of the children with a unique brand of true concern, asking no donation.
They can turn the frown of a child around into a smile, simply by sparking that child's imagination;

They enable our children to grow in a positive light, through
friendship and information.
They try to give a child the helping hand needed, to successfully
succeed with determination;
They assist our youth in developing and attaining, a genuine
sense of motivation.
They afford the child and the parents extra personal time, in the
form of a short vacation;
They give their love to the children, freely, of an extraordinary
quality, without charge nor question.
They want our youths to have a chance to reach their potential,
void the negative temptation;
They do care for the kids and that's a blessing in disguise,
deserving the public's cooperation.
They know there's no way a child's dreams, wants, and needs,
can be a sequenced systemization;
They too become a child and the child too gains a friend,
making for a natural euphoric combination.
They have chosen to work with our children to pursue
happiness, omitting any limitation;
They, the Big Brothers and Sisters, provide a service needed to
help upgrade our civilization.

HOSTAGE

Amen . . . , the echo from my ear bounced numb against my
brain;
A slew of butterflies flew to the roof of my stomach, paralyzed
I sat motionless unaware of any pain.
I felt the very air evaporate from my lungs within, my chest a
hole had become my every pore.
Pins and needles overpowered the back of my neck, my memory
said, "Stop," I've tasted this horror before.

Oh God! Please help me, please, I can't take anymore; tears
flushed my eyes from against my muscle flex;
A cold chill raced through me clotting my free-flowing blood,
oh, God, please don't put me to the test;
Though immensely tense and rigid, my muscles wavered as a
flag, my nerves were volcanic, I had lost control;
My energy and strength fled their prospective post,
"powerlessness" flashed in my mind, body and soul.

Death was the replacement that went about picking up the reins,
"helplessness" became the banner of my will.
"Obey" was the tune and beat of my drum; I must be dreaming
or something, this can't be for real.
Where's the police? The law? The justice that I've paid for?
Hell, I don't have to deal with this situation.
With indignance I glared searching for a weakened sign, only to
find that it was I who gripped domination.

Inside I ached of a rotten passion that ate my only soul, I wanted
to scream out as loud as I could.
I begged my intellect for a chance to make one last stand; yet,
contracting with death I wondered if I would.
A series of past events and deeds reeled through my mind, I felt
my fault for maybe not seeing the signs.
I wished I were a magician to escape this reality, somehow, I
constantly find myself in these binds.

I was bombarded with pains and sensitivities from within my
chest, I honestly expected my heart to fail.
My bladder felt inflamed as a balloon on the verge of exploding,
while still, I sat balanced on my own nail.
Death, really came as no surprise as I stared into its eyes, then
"Flash" . . . the wage.
I lay in my bed motionless gazing at today through my window.
I thanked God, for last night I was held hostage.

NUCLEAR WAR

We the people of the world, we can't take anymore;
We find ourselves on a head-on collision with nuclear war.
Nuclear war is upon us, you can see it more day by day;
If we don't unite to stop it, we will all be blown away.
We the people must agree on what is our common enemy;
And how to fight to stay free of a nuclear tragedy.
Nuclear War is on our doorstep, ready to knock down the door;
We must act now to prevent it, we must strike at its core.

We the people of the world, we can't take anymore;
We find ourselves on a head-on collision with nuclear war.
Nuclear war is upon us, you can see it more day by day;
If we don't unite to stop it, we will all be blown away.
We want our children free of the pain, suffering, and misery;
We want to give them the same opportunity to have a family.
We must contact our leaders, and let them know how we feel;
Make them understand that to us, nuclear war is for real.
Time is at hand, everyone is in fear;
Nuclear war could possibly be this year.

We the people of the world, we can't take anymore;
We find ourselves on a head-on collision with nuclear war.
Nuclear war is upon us, you can see it more day by day;
If we don't unite to stop it, we will all be blown away.
We must pick up the telephone, write a letter, send a telegram;
We must let our feeling be known throughout the land.
The time is now at hand, we all have seen the signs;
A nuclear war just might, destroy all of mankind.

We the people of the world, we just can't take anymore;
We find ourselves on a head-on collision with nuclear war;
Nuclear war is upon us, you can see it more day by day;
If we don't unite to stop it, we will all be blown away.

GRATITUDE

While visioning my seizing grasp onto the gates of Hell, the
soothing helping hand of A.A. was there.
Just as my loosely held last breath was about to expire, the
spirited helping hand of A.A. was there.
When I was trapped in an illusion and reaching for a delusion,
the real helping hand of A.A. was there.
As my very last teardrop descended from the corner of my right
eye, the replenishing hand of A.A. was there.
While huddled on a manhole cover seeking only to close my
eyes, the comforting hand of A.A. was there.
I was floating on a cloud when a sudden gust up and dethroned
me, the safety netted hand of A.A. was there.
I was abandoned and lonely as a child; I had no family to
belong, the clan and the hand of A.A. was there.
I had fallen through the depths of insanity I knew not who nor
what I was, the reassuring hand of A.A. was there.
When the cup a my soul overflowed with euphoric faith to which
I gave a rock, the inspired hand of A.A. was there.
While my brain and my eyes were aflamed in the gasoline of
rage, the extinguishing hand of A.A. was there.
On those earthquake mornings when my mobility was
impossible, the steady solid hand of A.A. was there.
I was sick and tired of being sick and tired; my health had
faded, the nourishing hand of A.A. was there.
I was fearful of being a real human being; trust, love, and risk,
how; the mortal hand of A.A. was there.
As all my life's possessions and works ran as water through my
hands, the spongy hand of A.A. was there.
Meekness, uniqueness, restless, breathless, fright, and fight
froze me; until the coaxing hand of A.A. was there.

Anguish, anger, distress, danger, and confusion confined me;
until the understanding hand of A.A. was there.
The helping hand of A.A. gave me a whole new life, rebirth!
Today I see the sun, I smell jasmine in the air.
The helping hand of A.A. took away my number giving me a
name, the lie tied to my tongue has been voided by prayer.
The helping hand of A.A. has lead me in the direction to my
Higher Power, my many lost steps have finally found their
food.
The helping hand of A.A. gave me back to me, "it's a miracle,"
yes, here in these rooms I've learned much about gratitude.

J.W.'S CHRONICLE

You were among the first to volunteer to go to battle, in defense
of your country and fellow man.
You offered your skills, you laid your life on the line, for seven
years you obeyed orders and the battle plan.
You tirelessly worked long hours most often maintaining two
jobs, to support your wanted family.
You sacrificed many years of your life to push your children
ahead, through all the seasons, everyday.
You were a proud individual and still are today, some instrument
could always be found in your hand.
You earned your money the old fashioned way, and you intended
to do so through your entire life span.
You were always there when I really needed you the most, to
my aid, for my protection you would come a runnin'.
You knew how to read my face to uncover my troubles, you
would cheer me up with answers, jokes and funnin'.
You didn't really go out for sports or many outdoor activities,
but I do remember going crabbing "surprise."
You never related to my false hatred when chastising me for my
wrongs, but only true love filled my teary eyes.

You and I even went to work together, you showed me
responsibility, you explained how a real man should think.
You and I hung out together with your friends and had fun,
many times from the same bottle we would drink.
You always told me to be independent by walking on my own
two feet, now I feel that was truly a mistake.
You are partially right, but none can walk alone, by leaning in
that direction many years the habit's hard to break.
You gave about as much of yourself to your family as anyone,
your youngest child today is a mature adult.
You enabled each child to sanely choose their own course;
without you, who could tell the result?
You know how difficult it is to express a hidden emotion,
expression, after years times years of subversion.
You aren't an island though you may feel like you are inside,
this can bridge through a unified conversion.
You carried me on your shoulders when I couldn't carry myself,
I had "big fun" continuously in your love.
You now need to be carried, it's my turn to carry you, with you
on my back we'll fly the skies like a dove.

REALITY

For over two and a half years I've paced tirelessly, to distance
myself from the hell wince I came;
Through the heavy snows in the mountain, through the hot
desert heat, through the cold marshy wilderness in the rain.
My energy being fueled by a serenely beauteous dream, the
view I held entrenched in my mind;
This dream was the nourishment I consumed along the way, I
dined daily, I was healthy, I felt fine.
I carried not fare nor luggage yet I journeyed first class, through
the lips of my soul my heart did sing;
My spirit was comforted in sheer luxury as I strolled with this
dream, I felt the flavor reserved for a king.

Nither fear nor problem united could muster to challenge my
peace, though I have seen, I still did not see;
This dream controlled my eyes for to it I gave control, my only
effort was walking and I felt so delightfully free.
My ego and pride lay dormant low below my knees, my faith
became the navigator of my destiny;
My enthusiasm flickered intently quaking the depths of my
existence, an emotional high that was void in my memory.
This choice dream had become my home, my love, this love
refreshed itself continuously as I gave it to all;
Materialization held little weight within the realm of this
existence, thus most the stumblings of life I'd not befall.
Suddenly the earth quaked destructively, I paused gazing the
terrain, whole mountains tumbled with bouldery and debris;
Great trees fell exploding the forests as do the bombs of war, in
shock and with tear "how could this happen to me."
Waiting for the dusted rubble to settle seemed timeless, but
when it did I could only feel this bland piercing dismay;
My heartbeat thrashed the walls of my throat, I gasped searching
for my dream, fear and failure threatened with foray.
Oh my dream . . . my dream . . . I bellowed, unable to see
beyond the rubble, I felt helplessness in face of doom and
gloom;
Was this my destined reward? Was this the end of my
progression? Surely sadness will come to open that old
wound.
I humbled myself upon a rock and I prayed to my Higher Power,
deeply hoping for a sign or some suggestion;
While standing I noted at my feet a reflection of the dream I so
treasured, I realized "I" had been focusing in the wrong
direction.

CRACK . . . PRO? OR CON?

Crack gives you an electrified sparkling high
It's super sensuous, unique, it's the ultimate high
For about thirty dollars a hit that you feel for about twenty
  minutes
To spend hundreds a day? I can see why

Crack is a habit forming addictive drug more powerful than man
Crack is a master over the human soul
Crack demands constant attention, worship and sacrilege
The more you give tighter becomes its hold

Crack gives you an electrified sparkling high
It's super sensuous, unique, it's the ultimate high
Crack will make you lie, fight your logic and overpower your
  instincts
Affording no opportunity to ask why

Crack's facade ends up in smoke and so does your life,
Your valuables and your time
Crack will crack the picture you always thought of as life
Into sitting in jail alone, confused, without a dime

Crack gives you an electrified sparkling high
It's super sensuous, unique, it's the ultimate high
Crack will suspend you in a plastic space of "no rational"
Helplessly you're binded to fear and failure, why?

Crack's process can be as explosive as a pinless grenade
Crack can and will explode your very heart
Crack has turned the strongest and smartest into mere puppets
Humiliatingly dehumanizing is its only art

Crack gives you an electrified sparkling high
It's super sensuous, unique, it's the ultimate high
Crack's euphoric high can only be attained once per lifetime
So to repeatedly attempt the unattainable—why?

Crack is an absolute dream with no base in reality
Nightmares usually travel through sleep
Crack becomes the shepard there's no room for our true GOD
Thus the poor user becomes crack's sheep

Crack gives you an electrified sparkling high
It's super sensuous, unique, it's the ultimate high
Crack may thrill, it surely will kill, forceably cause blood to
spill
It'll take your will and take your "Jill"—why?

For about thirty dollars a hit that you feel about twenty minutes
Crack destroys the cells in your brain
Crack gives of fame, in reality it's just the flames
At best you'll roam through life not knowing anything

MEMORIAL DAY

We in this blessed land of the brave, of the free
Of the courageous, of GOD, of humanity
Yes, we have set aside a special time—in our minds
In our hearts, in our lives, in our prayers, in memory

Through sorrow we found praise, through chaos found love
Through death we grasp forgiveness—any way
The moment is at hand when upon our gratitude we all stand
To pay tribute for peace, it's MEMORIAL DAY.

The magnitude of the deed, extracting fruit from weed
A task beyond the reins of the great at kings' commands
One by one they came and signed, their patriotism equally shined
An energy treasured by all kinds of man

Fearless and fearful was the blend, brave and bravish both spent
Coherent the silent decree we must obey
The essence of true liberty they maintained—some gripped heroism
Some gripped pain, they all equal one this MEMORIAL DAY

Into the darkness of uncertainty they wilfully plunged
The earth consumed their blood like a sponge, yet they marched on
An aspect of their duty was to learn to sing—to themselves,
Their foes and through everything—they blew their horn

"Give me liberty or give me death," set me free or take my breath
For it is only to my Maker that I now pray
Their dreams are today's reality, their deeds the base of our morality
Thus we remember MEMORIAL DAY

Task, achievement, and completion was and still is the goal
Overcoming struggles brings a happy success
Endurance, perseverance and persistence are the tools they used
Those who have fallen we pray GOD will bless

A dream is only a dream if we allow it to remain a dream
Words without action equals no pay
Amid the reality of the freedoms and liberties we enjoy today
We humbly offer our praise this MEMORIAL DAY

Viewing our American history in retrospect, in silence
I see many aspects if within my power I would change
The hurts, the tears, the injustice, suffering, confusion, misery
But if I did—would I yet be the same?

Together we must unite to overcome adversity we must stand
Hand in hand—together our hope will not stray
Together with our hearts, with our dreams and aspirations
We remember all our fraternity on MEMORIAL DAY

EDUCATION VS SPORTS

Escaping was my most shrilling scream of pure pain
Then out I went like a light
I was involved in what was described as a
Massive sports collision, no one knew of my plight

Each time I drifted back to consciousness
The pain would again come and take me away
Through tears grievingly my "Pro" dreams reeled
Beyond my reach, Oh GOD it's such a high price to pay

Upon my next flash of reality I saw my coach and a nurse
It was the hospital I could tell from the smell
With panic I clawed at his hand for fear now totally
Controlled me, upon my face was where his tears fell

Then again the intense pain plunged me into the darkness
I had no light to help me to find my way
I was lost and alone in a space I had never known
As if a statue, I had no feelings nor memory

Later, I was told I had been in a coma for several days
But to me it was like I was in a weird dream
My Mom cried when she saw me smile while still under
My guess is it gave more room for her hope to cling

I saw myself paused on the steps overwhelmed in joy as
I gazed the landscape of my new campus
Sheer happiness had nearly taken my breath away
My smile seemed to widen with each pound in my chest

I clinched my fists while shouting out silently:
"I'm really here, this is my dream come true."
Skill and opportunity had truly blessed me with this day
My sun boldly shined, my skies so blue

Passing grades in my classes was a breeze, I was a "Jock"
Sport practice consumed my everyday
In addition, exercise and travel extracted my hours
Somehow void of true pride, I found graduation day

Yet in the world of pro ball with the glitter, big money and
Fame, I made it and had the zeroes as proof
I was lucky and I knew it to have such a career
Because my degree was not fit even for minor use

As I opened my eyes for the first time in days on my own power
All the faces I did recognize, though vague
We engaged in a massive hug, their tears were of happiness and joy
Mine was because I had no feeling in my leg

"HUMBLE"

Oh Lord, it's so hard to be humble, it gets much harder to be
humble everyday,
Oh Lord, it's so hard to be humble, please take my hand and
show me the way,
I've learned that to mumble is not being humble, I'll not allow
fear to dictate to me,
I've learned that meekness does not mean weakness, it's merely
a sign of my faith in thee,
I've learned through your guidance I can excel, by being humble
I can stand next to you,
I've learned there's no uprising that you can't quell, in my
meekness my troubles have no hue,

Oh Lord, it's so hard to be humble, it gets much harder to be humble everyday,
Oh Lord, it's so hard to be humble, please take my hand and show me the way,

Every morning I'm met by adversity, I respond by attaching as I have done in the past,
My automatic reply is to fight to the end, I have a fear for losing and coming in last,
Then I become so ashamed of myself, for not practicing what I've learned and what I know,
I realize how difficult it is to be humble along the way, no matter in which direction I go,
Oh Lord, it's so hard to be humble, it gets much harder to be humble everyday,
Oh Lord, it's so hard to be humble, please take my hand and show me the way,

In all of my daily prayers I pray for forgiveness, for direction, guidance, strength, and hope,
I honestly try to begin my every morning anew, by reviewing my prayer and the words I spoke,
As a knight in shining armor hoping to serve you Lord, I see in no way I'll end retreating,
But as the day grows older the pebbles become boulders, it becomes me, the day is defeating,
Oh Lord, it's so hard to be humble, it gets much harder to be humble everyday,
Oh Lord, it's so hard to be humble, please take my hand and show me the way.

"MY LOVE"

The Farmer is very happy, when he sees the rain fall upon the land,
Knowing most of the seeds he planted, soon tall from the earth, they will stand,

When the threat of drought is upon the people, they scurry to
hoard water in jars,
Then finally, when the rain falls they're so elated, knowing the
water will fill the reservoirs,
As the heat from the hot summer sun, is on the verge of
destroying the flowers,
Mother Nature will step in to protect them, by drenching the
earth with showers,
The Fisherman loves to go fishing in the rain, as it falls into the
sea,
He catches more than enough which enables him, to feed more
than just his family,
When I'm not there with you when you awake, and you feel
lonely and blue,
Just remember these words I'm giving to you, until I get back
they'll see you through,
And the words are: Each and every rain drop that falls from up
above,
Is just a mere symbol of, My Love, My Love, My Love.
Where would a leaf be without a branch that's still connected to
a tree?
How could the fish and other mammals survive, without water
in the sea?
Without water, no form of life as we know it, could make it on
its own,
There's never been a heartbeat nor emotion, ever found to be in
a stone,
Plants pollinate all through the night, sending moisture through
the air way up high,
Evaporation is another way of sending, the moisture back up
into the sky,
Water is so very important to us all, we hope it should always
be around,
Mankind can't mass produce it's water, we must wait until it
falls to the ground,
All of the water on this planet fell from the Heavens, in the
form of rain,
Look at all the happiness we get from it, to feel sadness is really
a shame,
That's why I say to please remember: Each and every raindrop
that falls from up above,
Is just a mere symbol of, My Love, My Love, My Love.

BERGENFIELD

Should I have to face death today, I'd not shed a tear, for within
the relm of my Higher Power I'd somewhere be;
My LORD said "my Father has many many, many rooms in
His mansion, and in His Kingdom He will have lodging
for me."
My inherited fear of death has been taken away and been
replaced with joy, just to be near His Righteousness is my
life's desire;
To exist under the rule of my GOD is everything I ever wanted,
in His Kingdom I would most graciously retire.
Death is not mine to give or take, I can only hope for
acceptance, it's used as a final tool in this life;
Who am I to end my own life? Does it solely belong to me?
What is the payment? What is lifes value, and to whom do I
pay what price?
I can remember blaming my parents and cursing the day I was
born, I was misunderstood and hurting, "the world wouldn't
change for me;"
I thought I was a burden to everyone, I thought my pain would
last forever, I thought my life held no value, I was so lonely.
I felt intense alarming confusion, I was lost in my community,
who could I tell or trust, to explain my internal feeling?
I searched my entire conscious for an answer, I even begged for
help, but all the answers avoided me and my questions just
kept reeling.
Reality slapped my face leaving a burning sensation, I cried
with helplessness because I had no defense;
I was a number I had lost my name, I had no identity of my
own, my future seemed so vague, bland, and dense.

Alcohol and Drugs wasn't an answer, they merely prolonged my pain, the sickness and taste were vile to my being;
But I truely needed an escape for life's pressures are overbearing, the thought of GOD, I knew not the meaning.
Would suicide really tell the world that I didn't want to play?
Did I expect to get even? Would I get the last laugh?
Who would I hurt the most? My parents? My teachers? I have no real friends, for a few weeks I'll have all attention, then that too will pass.
But what about me? Where will I go? What will I become? Would I be punished or banished? would I still feel shame?
DEATH is NOT the answer, it's true meaning escapes my mind, through life there's GOD, hope, love, and growth yet to claim.
Today, I realize that the entire world and life as I perceive it, exists entirely within the relms of my own mind;
Life will NEVER stay the same, for each new day will bring new change. So, every problem I face WILL pass, as I grow through time.

SUNSHINE

There are many, many different ingredients to beauty and love; that can't always be seen crystally clear.
This love and beauty go hand and hand as one; like the individual seasons I enjoy during the year.
Beauty lays comfortably abundant, in my every vision; at my every sighting, my glance, and my gaze.
Love is the bare truth inspiring my feelings deep inside; love is expressed in so many different ways.
Beauty is in the eye of the beholder, it depends on "see;" the light is mine to do with as I please.
As each season unfolds releasing it's own unique display; they are all united through their one source of energy. . . .
I can see a beautiful autumn day, with a clear crisp blue sky; with all the colors and multicolored leaves.

I see the bold green pastures and fields in the distance; I see the
doe and deer peeking through the trees.
I can see the beauty of winter in a sparkling crystal freeze;
dominating my view from head to toe.
I see the frost on my window, that really tells me it's cold; I see
that happy smiling snowman in the snow.
I can see a beautiful spring morning without a cloud in the sky;
birds a singing, buds a sprouting, harmlessly.
I see children laughing and playing, I can feel the kid inside
of me.
I see the rain falling gently, ever so gingerly.
I can see the beauty of Mother Nature basking in the summer;
with all the little creatures, it's quite a flair.
I see through the clear water of the stream at the fish inside; I
see butterflies, I smell Jasmine in the air.
Sunshine, Oh Sunshine, you are my love; if only I could express
the joyment I receive from your rays.
In the darkness of night through my imagination; I can still feel
your warmth in many, many different ways.
Your soothing soft touch really rings my bell; for your glow
continuously lightens up my everyday.
On those cold chilly winter nights when I miss you the most; I
yet can visit with you, in my memory.
All forms of life as I know it seems dependent upon your
presence; I rely upon you more than words can say.
I so love standing before you, the thrill is all mine; Sunshine,
Oh Sunshine, your the beauty of love in my everyday.

FREEDOM IS MY ONLY CHOICE

Freedom, oh sweet freedom, please take my hand; for truely
you are my salvation.
Rigorous are my constant attempts to retain you; at moments it
is for you that I grip starvation.

Equality and freedom do march to the same drummer; they both
have that unique synchronization.
Everyday I stride with freedom, step for step, but I tire; thus I
regret our eventual separation.
Discharging from bondage whether physical, mental, or
spiritual; deserves much credit and salutation.
Obstacles along the way can be conquered by faith; my Higher
Power can topple any situation.
Momentous is the fact that I can choose not to be alone,
freedom gives me this stipulation.

Insufficiency consumed my control, it overpowered my will;
freedom, I summized a mere fluke.
Succumbing to lifes negatives only bought me tears; for me, all
the pain and shame became absolute.

My liberty was definitely caged, my dreams held anchor; my
every inhale was sifted and drawn.
Yellow was my banner, born through fruitless confrontation; I
was ridiculed and looked upon with scorn.

Openly true freedom stood before me beckoning; yet bewildered,
I still extended my hand.
Naturalness had overwhelmed my every emotion to retreat; now
freedom gazed upon a naked man.
Liberty had completely filled the cup of which I had become;
honor and pride glowed in my eyes.
Youth transformed my logic, my knowledge, and my soul; I
honestly held freedom in my hand, void disguise.

Clear is my mind to pursue what ever turns me on; if I can
perceive the dream, I can attain.
Hallowed is the energy to which I am connected; my quests and
horizons are unrestrained.
Outspoken is my heart among the mankind of this world; for I
am now a lamb of my Higher Power.
Independent is my faith to scale throughout the atmosphere;
though I remain as rooted as the flower.
Costlessly I partake of the love, only found in freedom; where
monetary values, just do not exist.
Emancipation means freedom from bondage, in all its faces;
GOD inspired emancipation, is the gift.

NEW YEARS EVE

This morning my thoughts are to run, flee, escape, of
abandoning ship; fearfully, I recall feeling this way before.
Seems in every direction I look my treasured hope has faded; I
feel such pressure, I just can't take much more.
I'm only human, and I'm weak, my past misery I refuse to
repeat; yet, I possess no solutions or suggestions.
The one light left in my life is from the Heavens above; If not
for GOD in my life, I'd choose death with no questions.
I believe in looking before I leap, but I see nowhere to land; I'm
dangling dangerously at the edge of my rope.
I've gained the love, pride, respect, and friendship, from myself
and others; who would truely believe I find it difficult to
cope?
Realizing that I was at an emotional relapse at any moment; I
shutter to close my eyes for being caught out of lifes flow.
"If I had your hand, I'd turn mine in", how many times I've
been told? but this morning I awake in a space not of my
control.
My very first awareness was "Fear," my heart pounded wildly;
where am I? How did I get here? What was happening
to me?
I felt I was encircled, I was caught helpless in the middle; I
searched the flames for hope, but of it I could not see.
From the pit of my stomach panic began to churn and rumble;
the tears filled my eyes as sorrow entered blanketing my
heart.
Disappointment took my hand and roughly embraced me; my
tears fell to the dance floor one by one, from it I couldn't
pull apart.

The open roads I saw was death, and they were no bargain;
when it came to conscious suffering and pain, I'd cower.
I had awaken moments ago, then like magic "Zap" I was here;
I honestly believe in this "space" I wouldn't last the hour.
I had no options, I could only stand and serve, no remembrance
to retreat; as defeat marched by, I watched from the viewing
stand.
Numb was now the sensation filling my pores, plickling my
skin; a serious neon "help" flashed through my mind, yet, I
had no plan.
Subconsciously my hand darted out and retrieved pen and paper;
my last hope was GOD, my Higher Power, so I wrote to
HIM a letter.
I sent out that s.o.s., detailing my plight and condition; I then
picked up the phone and reached my Rehab., I felt so much
better.
When I finally looked back to myself, I had traveled to a more
comfortable space; I thanked GOD I was away from that
infernal.
I wiped the sweat from my brow in the dark silence, at the edge
of my bed; I realized, through my Higher Power, "Hope
Springs Eternal."

SHARING

This morning I received a telephone call from Susi my good
friend; in the past we have experienced many similar
emotional expressions.
Today we can look back at Hell and euphoricly laugh aloud
together; yet, still we don't know the answers to the vast
questions.

She invited me to share with her in the joy we both lived; she said a few of her other friends would also drop by.
I never could say no to a Lady, my automatic "yes" escaped me; unconcerned with any of the details I said yes I'll really try.
As I replaced the receiver I detected a serene tingling within me; it was a beautiful feeling of calm and a rewarding peace.
Indirectly I began preparing for our rendezvous as I went about my day; for today Susi would deliver the medicine I need for my disease.
I caught myself smiling a few times while pondering our conversation; I unconditionally trust her honesty, as she too with me.
Hey, its Spring, love has descended and I feel electrified; tonight my heart will direct my happiness pleasurably.
She greeted me at the gate, she tenderly clutched my hand; she said welcome, she smiled, she had those stars in her eyes.
This dwelling was a massive fortress, it completely consumed my view; but just being in her presence elimated all of the whys.
She lead me up through a chamber, I heard the door slam behind me; but I only sensed positives flowing throughout the atmosphere.
She lead me to a desk where I was introduced and exchanged hello's; then on into a room when she said: "girls he's here!."
WOMEN!, and me? All these pretty ladies and me with no competition! what a surprise, I was gaping, the reality nearly blew my mind.
I smiled, I glanced, and made room for them all on my pink cloud; then for the next few hours we all seemed exempt of time.
We feast on pure love, acceptance, identification, and friendship; we drank an abundance of laughter, truth, and smiles.
We all became as one and we looked at ourselves fearlessly; even the Bee buzzing about joined in on our style.
All my life I have always loved all women, I was born that way; but my insane disease lusted for the wrong pleasures and things.
But now I can still love all women as I do myself, we're GOD'S creation; this is one of the invaluable gifts that true faith brings.

Our gathering was coming to an end for time had found us;
so we hugged, we prayed, and we hugged, it was time to set sail.
Outside Susi and I exchanged our good-bye's, we parted in love and said: Lets try to meet here again next week at Northhampton County Jail.

LIFE

I thought the meaning of life would be found through conquering; so down the path I stroad.
I thought the perception of life sparkled from diamonds and gold; so hurredly I traveled down that road.
I thought I saw the true essence of life from atop a mountain; so I brought up the land in the valley.
I thought that I could purchase life through material things; so I purchased more wares than I could carry.
I thought if I sought life intently both night and day; that surely I would overtake its steps.
I thought life was elusive but yet a game I could win; thus I would receive all of its assets.
I thought life was cruel so I openly welcomed a raging frustration; which I reaped sadness, tears, and inequity.
I thought life was unattainable always lying just beyond my reach; so I persued and acquired insanity.
Why, why, why, was my constant cry; I had no answers, did I miss the meaning? I was confused.
I would cry in my beer and try to drown myself in spirits; the drugs I never used I only abused.
Hope, I could not spell, to me growth was limited to the forest; I was entombed in all my little sins.
helplessness, hopelessness, and powerlessness was my three emotions; my existence was a waste from end to end.
I thought life was based on luck or inheritance; all I ever wanted was happiness, is it a fantasy?

I thought life was to be chased twenty-four hours a day; but just
the thought killed all my energy.
I thought life would be mine through family, children, and
employment; so how did I become a drunken bum.
I thought life came from the Sun, I know I surely received its
rays; what happened to me? what have I become?
Through gentle positive rehabilitation I received loving direction;
with suggested hope for life through A.A.
A.A. gave me all the happiness I ever wanted, and more; now I
enjoy my life with everyone everyday.
To me life is as a thousand piece puzzle and I'm only one piece;
focusing on my one piece, does not lifes picture make.
I can only position myself on lifes board and accept being as
happy as I can;
with faith and GOD, todays life I most graciously take.

HEAVENLY FATHER

Thank you, oh thank you my Heavenly Father; please hear the
song of my praise.
Repeatedly I've offered to You my thanks in my yesterdays; for
I receive Your gifts everyday.
To count all my blessings seems an impossible task; yet, I'm
only viewing my last few years.
My heart does shine as the sun inside; my faith has matured,
only pure happiness fills my tears.
You were there for me always when I wasn't there for myself;
You brought me home when I couldn't see.
I chose to exist for months without any proper diet; still, I
received healthy nourishment miraculously.
For years I sat content on my log at the edge of lifes path;
intently staring at an illusion upon the earth.
Without conscious, hope, direction, trust, and compassion; I
thought of worthlessness but You gave me rebirth.

Patience has befriended me, through humiliation I realized
power; I found kindness in the joy of giving.
A hug, a kiss, a smile, a handshake, and a warm reassuring
love; I realize lifes meaning isn't in surviving, its in the
living.
I've had many bad days in my life and too few good ones; now
my days are filled with goodness and growth.
I was insane, obscene, my self worth held no esteem; today I
have character and acceptance and I love them both.
For me, You accomplished all the things I couldn't for myself;
and then on to beyond my dreams of dreams.
A blissful laughter bellows from the depths of my soul, my
smile is real; seems like ages when my voice only held
screams.
You have given me the ultimate treasure, myself to me; my value
more precious than anything determined by man.
What have I done to deserve such Grace? what deed did I
perform? but who am I to question Your plan.
Thank you, oh thank you my Heavenly Father; please hear the
song of my praise.
Your wish is my desire, my hope is to be able to fulfill Your
Will; You have rewarded me in many splendid special ways.
Life is beautiful its for the living, the giving, and the sharing;
emiting happiness, euphoria, and serenity.
My faith in You has illuminated my spirit and perception of life;
my loyalty to You will outlast infinity.

SOBRIETY PRESS is a book publishing firm, based on truth, patience, honesty, courage, trust, "enthusiasm", and that old work ethic: "a hard day's work, for a fair day's pay". We deliver success! The following people, groups, organizations, federal and state agencies, educational communities, and business concerns have each helped in carrying the fundamental bricks needed to build the foundation of SOBRIETY PRESS. To the following we offer our most elevated praise for your solid, gentle, and replenishing support.

Nick C.
Blanche Angen
Gordon H.
Gene M.
Anna Wilson
Frank L. Ahart, 3rd
James McG.
Annie P.
John and Mike, Dreamland
Dr. C. A. Ravanzo
April Erzak
Frankie S., B&L Lunch
Jack D.
Charlie K. and Larry
Barry Mueller
Bob R.
Debra Holloway
Lee Holmes
L. H. Naumann
William Brown
Clyde Lewis

Mrs. Nancy Reagan, First Lady
Ronald Reagan, U.S. President
Thomas H. Kean, N.J. Governor
U.S. Dept. of Health and Human Services, Centers of Disease Control
N.J. Dept. of Health, Div. of Alcoholism
N.J. Commission For The Blind
M.A.D.D., National Headquarters
The American Red Cross
Thomas F. Vezzetti, Mayor-Hoboken, N.J.
Summer Festival '86
Arthur J. Holland, Mayor-Trenton, N.J.
The Phoenix House, N.Y., N.Y.
Big Brothers/Big Sisters of Warren Co.
The Easton Express
The Hunterdon Poets
The National Rainbow Coalition, Inc.
The Statue Of Liberty Foundation, Inc.
The Washington Educational Community
The White House
Thomas Reed, Attorney

David Schiff
Kathy P.
Danny
John S.
Eddie S.
Brooklyn Harry
M. Flood, Principal
John James, PSE&G
Susi B.
Bruce P. Frassinelli, Easton Express
Roganne S.
Rev. D. A. Klemens
Matt M.
Rev. Lawrence Durham
Dr. Lorraine Catania, Life Saver
P. J. O'Malley, Superintendant
Kandace Threadgill
Kim E. Kobylus

and
The Entire Staff Of MARWORTH

Miracles . . ., most POSITIVELY do exist, and persist. . . . . . .
Cliff W.

SPECIAL THANKS PAGE

I offer my most warm very special thanks to the following for their much appreciated and most important support, endorsement and/or kindness involved in making this "remote dream" a reality.

Nick C., President,
mentor, friend
Gordon H.
Frank L. Ahart, III
Anna Wilson
A.A.
April Nagy
James McG.
Cheryl
My Family
Dr. C. A. Ravanzo
Mike and John
Louis H. Naumann
New Jersey Department of
Health, Division of
Alcoholism
Mrs. Nancy Reagan,
First Lady
The American Red Cross
The White House
Thomas H. Kean,
Governor—NJ
The National Rainbow
Coalition, Inc.
The Statute of Liberty Ellis
Island Foundation, Inc.
NJ Department of
Health—Human Services
The Pheonix House
Big Brothers/Big Sisters of
Warren County
M.A.D.D.—National
Headquarters
Ronald Reagan, President
Delores B. Reilly, Counselor
Barry D. M.—Castle Press
Publications, Inc.
William Brown, Agent—North
Carolina Mutual

LOOK FOR THESE UPCOMING NEW EDITIONS TO BE RELEASED BY SOBRIETY PRESS PUBLICATIONS:

"METAMORPHOSE".
An Alcoholismistic Expression.

"EXCERPTS OF SOBRIETY".
An Alcoholismistic Expression.

and coming soon. . . . . ;

"SUCCESS", THE JOURNEY.
An Alcoholismistic Biography.

These titles will soon be available through Mail Order, or check with the Bookstores in your area.

For Publishing Information and Book Orders write to:

SOBRIETY PRESS
P.O. Box 201
Washington, N.J. 07882

Certain of our selections we have produced in our Poster Poem Versions, (13 3/8" by 11") with color boarders. These are now also available for $1.50 ea., plus $.50 for postage and handling. Please allow for 2 to 6 weeks for delivery.